# ETERNAL ANSWERS FOR AN ANXIOUS AGE

**Foreword by
William J. Byron, S.J.**

# Rev. Robert Paul Mohan

D1166214

Our Sunday Visitor, Inc.
Huntington, Indiana 46750

INTERNATIONAL STANDARD BOOK NUMBER: 0-87973-592-9
LIBRARY OF CONGRESS CATALOG CARD NUMBER: 85-60518

Cover design by James E. McIlrath

*Printed in the United States of America*

592

# Contents

Foreword / 7

Introduction / 8

The Priestly Vocation / 9

The Gambler / 13

Junk Ethics / 15

Disposables / 18

Pride / 20

Civility / 24

Freedom / 28

Fidelity / 32

Humor / 36

Special Moments / 39

Discouragement / 41

Forgiveness / 44

Weariness / 48

Belonging / 51

Ambiguity / 54

The Unholy Trinity / 56

Complexity / 59

Courage / 62

*Anger* / **65**
*Confidence* / **67**
*Death* / **71**
*The Fallen-Away* / **74**
*Reverence* / **76**
*Suffering* / **80**
*Anxiety* / **84**
*Caesar's Things* / **87**
*Responsibility* / **90**
*Joy* / **93**
*Loneliness* / **97**
*Mood of the Time* / **100**
*Humility* / **105**
*Sin* / **107**
*Insensitivity* / **111**
*Distant Christians* / **114**
*Sickness* / **117**
*Generosity* / **120**
*Authenticity* / **123**
*Faith* / **125**
*Toleration* / **129**

# Foreword

*A* month or two before I became president of The Catholic University of America in 1982, a lay trustee of the university sent me, with unmistakable delight and approval, a copy of a sermon he had heard at Sunday Mass in the Washington suburb of Potomac, Maryland. The preacher was Robert Paul Mohan — "a credit to our university," said the trustee in his handwritten endorsement.

Since then, many warmly appreciative comments on Father Mohan's homilies have come to my attention. People who have heard him preach encouraged him to gather some of his sermons together into this book.

The preacher, indeed "a credit to our university," is a priest, philosopher, professor, and gentleman. This book is thoughtful, instructive, and gentle in its invitation to the better life.

Early in my reading of these chapters, I began to track: "principled living," "principled intelligence," "principled behavior," "the principled life." The writer is a man of principle calling believers to reflect on Gospel principles that will not only guide but also change their lives.

Knowing the context in which these essays originated, and knowing many of the persons who have been touched by them, I feel justified in offering a suggestion to the reader. These chapters are brief, clear, and very well written. Resist the temptation to read more than one at a time. Resist also the natural tendency to read them alone. It would be enormously beneficial, I suspect, if members of a family who typically worship together on Sunday take a few moments now and then to share not pew space but a chapter from this book, read aloud and reflected upon together. A review of the table of contents will reveal a list of many topics that should be discussed in Christian families. Robert Mohan frames that discussion in high style while grounding it in solid theological reflection.

*William J. Byron, S.J.*
PRESIDENT
THE CATHOLIC UNIVERSITY OF AMERICA

# Introduction

*T*HESE reflections are the outgrowth of homilies delivered at Our Lady of Mercy Church in Potomac, Maryland, over the last few years.

I should like to acknowledge the gracious hospitality extended to me there by Monsignor Vincent Gatto, Father Joseph Byron, and Father Michael Mellone.

I am particularly indebted to Joseph and Edna Lynott, Peter Plamondon, La Salle Caron, Stacey M. Weilandt, and Father William Byron, S.J., president of

The Catholic University of America, for their assistance in the preparation of this volume.

I have tried to be serious without being solemn, and hope that despite the informality of the approach, the life-enhancing strength of the "good news" may find its way into the lives of some of God's people.

*Robert Paul Mohan*
THE CATHOLIC UNIVERSITY OF AMERICA
MARCH 1, 1985

# The Priestly Vocation

*W*HEN the television mini-series *The Thorn Birds* first aired, there were some one hundred and ten million people who watched it. The four-part production was one of the most popular presentations in history, and, of course, featured the ambitious Father Ralph, his illicit romance, and the saga of the Cleary family.

Despite the theatricality, it provoked both frivolous and serious questions. As for the frivolous, one young lady said to me: "I never had a pastor who looked like Richard Chamberlain." Only gallantry prevented me from replying: "Not all parishioners look like Rachel Ward either."

But there are serious questions in an age in which infidelity is common. I wonder: Would the romance have had the same fascination if the hero were a banker or a lawyer? We never saw the ambitious Father Ralph doing anything priestly, and that's why I should like to use *The Thorn Birds* as kind of an introduction into the nature of the priestly vocation. Not only do we not ordinarily conceive of romantic archbishops, but people often go to the extreme of seeing the life of a priest as a bloodless neutering thing, and are perhaps more than a little interested when a priest exhibits the frailty of the human condition. But ours is a very human vocation. In Edmond Rostand's romantic play *Cyrano de Bergerac*, there is a scene under Roxanne's balcony, when a musician is to give alarm by playing a sad tune if a man approaches, or a merry tune if a woman approaches. He plays both confusedly, and who enters but a friar! The friar doesn't quite have an identity.

I think in our predominantly secular culture, we priests are often thought of that way. Our priesthood is of God; but we are men, and the Meggies of the world — as charming as they are — are not our greatest problem. By and large, we are happy men, as capable as our brothers in the world — as a recent study revealed — of dealing with people and forming friendships. But it's a tragedy that we who love our life and our mission as Christ's priests have failed to communicate the joy of serving Christ to the young men of this generation as an alternative human lifestyle, with its sacrifices and its joys.

When I was in Paris not too long ago as a houseguest of French friends, my hostess told me that very few priests were ordained for the archdiocese of Paris last year — in France, the eldest daughter of the Church!

And the situation is not much better here in the United States, or in Britain, or in Germany, or in Italy. Our culture, permissive and secular, has been sold on the myth that a single life cannot and should not be lived, that a celibate life could not possibly be happy. This is rubbish. I make no more generous sacrifices in life than my brother out in the secular world.

Despite what sociologists call the "eroticization of the social environment," a meaningful life has many values and many commitments, and an honorable man honors the commitments that he has made. But in choosing our lives, none of us leaves behind his humanity. Pride and charity and sensitivity can blind a priest as they blind other men; but the Lord, who used Peter as the building block of his Church (Peter, who thrice denied him), can use us. God can make worthy those whom he chooses.

Now, this may be an unnecessary concern, for our humanness may at times be all too evident. I can remember that a student of mine once said that he didn't feel obliged to give a good example to his son, because he didn't want the son to think he was some kind of a god. As tactfully as I could, I intimated that I really didn't think that this would be much of a problem.

The essential point I would like to make here is, of course, that our priestly vocation is simply a vocation for men. A man who cannot see the beauty of God's creation — and that includes the beauty of human love — has no place in the priesthood. If the giver sees no gift he brings to God, what indeed is he giving? If the one who serves, loves only the status and the ceremonies, he would do much better to become a politician or an actor.

The work of the Church, of course, must indeed go on — and it goes on in competition with an aggressive secularism which preaches indulgence rather than discipline, selfishness rather than concern, privilege rather than responsibility, and acquisition rather than generosity. The media of communication and entertainment are strong, articulate, and they preach much better than we do. And these are the voices being listened to. Theirs are the values being adopted and theirs the opportunistic morals being lived. Christ's apostle is once more a voice crying in the wilderness. A voice crying for principled living, loving concern, and spiritual values is being drowned out by louder voices — and, increasingly, the apostle is quite simply not there.

We do, indeed, need good priests, and I'm afraid that the real ones not only do *not* look like Richard Chamberlain, but most of them are not really worried about the bishop's purple or the cardinalitial red.

So I'm not concerned, really, that Father Ralph might have scandalized the faithful, though he was delinquent in more ways than one. I would be much more worried about a Father Ralph if he were a sour and mean old skinflint, locked up in a rectory, incapable of any kind of human love or sensitivity.

Let us all pray for vocations to a life that can indeed be a joy, and a life that is not prohibitively hard to him who freely chooses and faithfully executes. A life that touches people from birth to death in the most solemn moments of their lives; that rightly enjoins fidelity and finds joy in that fidelity; and a life that hears in moments of both joy and sadness the words of our Savior: "I will reward you a hundredfold and give you eternal life."

# The Gambler

$I_T$

has been said that the arts are sensitive barometers of our culture. Not long ago on a long drive I was listening to a ballad being sung by Kenny Rogers. It was a song called "The Gambler." The chorus points out that a gambler knows when to play or throw in a hand ("hold 'em" or "fold 'em," as the song goes). The gambler also knows "when to walk away" from a game, and "when to run." And I thought that in a way this song could be applied to prudence in the Christian life. Perseverance and patience in difficult situations require courage and staying power — knowing when to "hold 'em," in the Kenny Rogers idiom.

Knowing when to "hold 'em" means having confidence in our ability to do a job, live a life, fulfill a vocation, survive sorrow, and endure disappointment. Duty does place obligations upon us no matter how we feel, and we should depend upon the grace and strength of God to assist us in the living of a principled life even when it's difficult.

It's also true that we should know when to "fold 'em," know when to tailor our expectations to our abilities, know when a dream is to be realized, and when reality demands a more sober analysis and more modest expectation. This doesn't preclude legitimate risk, a gamble if you will; but we shouldn't try to bluff our way through life, pretending to possess skills and resources we do not have, deceiving others, doing injustice to others, being rude to others.

Sometimes it's not merely a question of determining conditions as much as a question of rising expectations. For instance, some people seem to think that they will live forever in this life. They think that death is something that happens only to somebody else. They never contemplate the most obvious of facts that, like others, they will die. Knowing when to "fold 'em," I think, means trying to see reality as it is and as it can be but realizing at the same time that fantasy should not encourage deliberate or inadvertent bluff.

Another line in this song is: "Know when to walk away." I can see this line too in terms of Christian prudence: walking away not only from the obviously sinful but also from the cheap and the shoddy; walking away from the second best, and the worthless, and the careless performance, and the thoughtless word, and the slovenly action.

And sometimes, we should indeed know when to run, both *to* something and *from* something — *to* that which must be done, and not avoided or deterred. And *from* something that may be a danger. Now is the acceptable time, Paul tells us. Some things demand our attention; others may compete for our attention. To the things that should be done and must be done for our natural or supernatural benefit, we should indeed run; and we should know when to run away too from more than mortal danger, not kidding ourselves that danger doesn't exist.

For instance, there is a Latin axiom, *"Obsta principiis"* ("Resist the beginnings"). Don't get involved.

Run — don't walk — to the nearest exit. For some reason, we don't talk about occasions of sin anymore, but we still have plenty of sin. And we still have plenty of proximate occasions of sin. And much of the misery that we bring upon ourselves could be avoided by recognizing the frailty of human nature — including our own — and acting with appropriate prudence. Sometimes that does mean inglorious flight.

Now, I'm not suggesting that you go looking for the paragons of the Christian life in country-and-western ballads, but in this whimsical moment I was struck by the perceived appropriateness of the gambling images. We should know when to "hold 'em" — and when to "fold 'em." We should know "when to walk away" — and "when to run."

# Junk Ethics

*O*CCASIONALLY in the past I have made it a point to discuss what I call junk ethics: a contemporary philosophy, or absence of it, in which a narcissistic obsession with self replaces divine or rational norms of human behavior. Right becomes what is convenient; duty is sneered at as rigorism; responsible behavior is ridiculed as both impossible and undesirable; and tradition, of course, is ridiculed as the experience of failure.

The differences of viewpoints are frequently highlighted but not necessarily embodied only by figures in the world of entertainment. For instance, in the recent past, tragically, John Belushi joined the sad ranks of Janis Joplin, Jimmy Hendricks, and Elvis Presley. Now, we can sympathize, of course, with truncated, messed-up lives; but I don't think it's uncharitable to look critically at the values that are represented.

These people are treated with a kind of cultic reverence. We have a kind of admiration for life in the fast lane, for outrageous behavior, antic irreverence, food fights, and wildness in general. Such figures are thought to have in our time a kind of endearing cuteness, despite the fact that the behavior in question is simply uncivilized and undisciplined.

One of our comedians — at this writing — has a film playing currently in no less than twenty-three area theaters. It's described by a *Washington Post* critic as incorrigibly funny. The man involved has a marvelous flair, despite the fact that he is constitutionally incapable of uttering a single English sentence without a dreary appeal to the three-word vocabulary of the street. And of course this relentlessly lavatorial style merely proves what has often been said — that this kind of language is the means by which the inarticulate give themselves the illusion of eloquence.

Now, we don't have to be flint-hard simplistic politicians of the moral majority to reject this junk. It's not surprising, I suppose, that this stuff goes on not only in the flamboyant world of entertainment but also in government, in business, in law, in education, and in private life. What is surprising, however, is that junk ethics today is almost expected in every sphere — from marital fidelity to international relations. And junk ethics is defended not only by the semiliterate but also by those who really should know better. We have all sorts of people standing around with smoking guns, so to speak, who say, "I didn't do anything wrong." We have unrepentant Watergate felons making the fast buck on the lecture circuit by saying that paranoia is the price of liberty.

We have junk ethics on the extremes of both right and left, and our immature of all ages have erroneously concluded that popularity and acceptability are equivalent to moral justification. And of course we have learned professors of ethics suggesting that right or wrong are merely subjective labels for our likes and dislikes.

I think the role of the Christian in all this is to assert the way of Christ, not in the antic enthusiasm of the fundamentalist, or in the crude illiteracy of the subway orator, but by a prayerful reflection and a grace-filled life, fortified by the sacraments and illuminated by informed human reason, and carried by us into our lives and into our world.

We have a big job to do as Christians today, and popularity has absolutely nothing to do with it. "I can do all things in him who strengthens me."

We should neither accept the junk values of our world nor be intimidated by them. The quiet firmness and strength of the man and woman of principle is a vocation. May we have the grace and the strength to make that vocation grow in our world.

# Disposables

*R*ECENTLY,
as I was flying back from London, I noticed how many
items — from newspapers to food containers, even
knives and forks — were disposable. We seem to think it
better to throw something away than wash it, or care for
it, or keep it. We've become the disposable society. We
even dispose of people — children before they're born,
old people by warehousing them when they clutter up
the neatness of our landscape. We dispose of moral principles when we find them inconvenient, rules when we
find them irksome, and responsibilities when we find
them crowding us and limiting our freedom.

I suppose the question might be asked, "Well, what
should the Christian regard as disposable or dispensable
in the living of the Christian life?" Now, I'm obviously
not talking about disposable cans and paper products or
the familiar detritus of our uses and indulgences. Certainly — for instance, at Lent and Advent — there are
times for considering what we can dispose of, or what excess baggage, physical and mental, we carry into this life
of ours.

One of the things our Lord seemed to emphasize was
a basically simple and uncomplicated life, and maybe
we should adopt an attitude to unnecessary involvement, and unnecessary possessions with which we sometimes complicate our lives. Perhaps we could dispose of
an activism that leaves little time for genuine family

life. A busyness oriented to success of the marketplace, and failure at home, and a busyness that's equivalent often to failure in prayer. Perhaps we could dispose of unwholesome and perhaps sinful associations, or those which are merely dangerous or frivolous. Perhaps we could dispose of a preoccupation with self that blinds us to others and their needs. Perhaps we could dispose of an anxiety that makes us fretful and unhappy, as if we didn't have faith in a provident God who loves us and knows our needs.

I think all of us feel at some time or other we simply get too caught up in things; and that's why — for instance, in any penitential season, or anytime during the year — we should call a halt. We should think and pray and trust more in God. Perhaps we could dispose of our sensitivity that makes us exaggerate slights and offenses, and results in estrangements from former friends, associates, and acquaintances. You know that kind of sensitivity is really pride — rotten pride — and it is an eminently disposable product, and we shouldn't even worry about recycling it.

Perhaps we could dispense with our indulgence and pampering of self, not only in obvious things like alcohol but also in the use of the necessities, real and imagined, and channel our sacrifices to the hungry and the starving in our midst. Perhaps we could dispose of uncharitable and unnecessarily critical speech — words that can wound, and those unpleasant and hostile silences that are as hurtful as words. And let's dispose of careless and sloppy performance as parents, as workers, as friends. And let's dispose of a whining and complaining demeanor that makes us martyrs to ourselves and bores to our friends. And let's dispose of the illusions that would tell us "to be popular is to be right," that "to be materialistic is to be realistic," and that "to be modern is to be faithless."

Let's dispose of anything that stands between us and God, between what we are and what we should be. And finally, let's dispose of the procrastination that would make or reform something tomorrow or next year. Maybe we won't be around tomorrow or next year.

So when we dispose of excess baggage, let us reaffirm our need of the indispensable and indisposable: living an active faith in the strength which is Christ Jesus.

# Pride

*W*HEN we read of Jesus warning against the hypocrisies and arrogance of the scribes and Pharisees, his condemnation of their strutting and seeking the first places in the synagogues and at banquets, his admiration for the poor widow — we are inclined to wonder whatever became of the vice of pride. Now, I'm not neglecting the humble theme of the widow's mite, for the custom of giving the equivalent of a mite has, I think, in our churches, been sedulously preserved, perhaps grudgingly, by people who wouldn't quibble to pay fifty dollars for a seat to see "Cats," or the same amount for a lunch at Lion d'Or.

It seems to me, however, that we don't hear much about pride anymore. One might wonder if it is because we've become more humble or simply more lax. Pride is very deceptive, because it's become a caricature vice. One thinks of the words of Oscar Wilde: "She is a peacock in everything but beauty." Pride conjures up strutting images of the arrogant and the pompous, uttering Lucifer-like defiances based on the exaggerated self.

The prideful figures are somewhat ridiculous, but I think really pride is much more subtle. It causes much more trouble in our daily lives than we are inclined to think it does, and it affects many people who would not dream that it's their problem.

Like all vices, pride is based on a falsification: a falsification of self, an inordinate self-love — a proper esteem that metastasizes into complete absorption with self; and it deals also with real or supposed privilege. It's a love affair that has no other; it's a form of worship that needs no God. One of Disraeli's detractors once said to him: "He is a self-made man and worships his creator." The prideful person is something like that. He can't really have mature relationships, can't get along with anyone for a long time, because his feelings are inevitably hurt.

Now, of course, pride *is* that vulgar boastfulness, that obvious arrogance with which we are all familiar: the braggart, the pusher, the boaster, the manipulator. But pride doesn't always speak so theatrically. It's not always obvious, and never really comic. It is a subtle evil that involves a loss of dependence on God, a minimizing of the needs and sensibilities of others with whom we associate on familial, professional, or social levels. It is a solar system in which we are the sun, and all must revolve around us or suffer our displeasure or estrangement.

What is extreme sensitivity if not pride? What is impatience if not pride? We all know people who have to be handled with kid gloves. They're affected by everything from a seating arrangement to the tone of a greeting. Is this really sensitivity of spirit? No, it's pride, rotten pride, childish pride.

Some would try to defend this, I suppose, on the ground it is solicitude for legitimate interest; but we know better, because sometimes we are the guilty party. How eloquent are those who despise gifts they don't possess, or even worse, those who fancy themselves as possessing the gift in question. That, of course, is not really pride but delusion.

There's a famous story of the man and wife who are seated in the parlor one evening; the husband is chomping on a cigar and looking very self-satisfied and says to his wife, "After all, there are few really great men in this world"; to which his wife says, somewhat acerbically: "Yes, and there happens to be one less than you think."

Now, as I say, not always does pride have this comic atmosphere, but let's take something like thoughtlessness. What is thoughtlessness if not pride? This is a supposedly innocent vice, but it's oxymoronic to say this! It is a vice and it is not innocent. No vice ever is. The thoughtless person is rarely thoughtless where his own interests are concerned. But if we thought others and their interests were really important, we wouldn't be thoughtless. Take the latecomer, the habitual forgetter of birthdays and anniversaries. He never forgets his own, of course. One of Rodney Dangerfield's great lines is about his twin brother who forgot his birthday.

What is the rationalization for everything from theft to adultery if not pride? The unwillingness to look at the self that is, and to criticize that self as to criticize others. Mirror, mirror on the wall, you are cruel to the proud man, because you reflect what is there to see, not what is imagined.

Pride is more like those amusement-park mirrors that distort, but distort only for the better. What is inordinate ambition, poisonous envy, vanity, presumption, and suspicion, if not pride? Even the success of others of our age and condition and profession becomes a reproach to the prickly self. I referred to Disraeli earlier. Nineteenth-century English history also produced two very strong characters in Gladstone and Cardinal Manning. There was a sensitivity between them which prompted Manning to say: "Mr. Gladstone is a substantive and likes to be attended by adjectives. I am not exactly an adjective."

Now, that's often our problem. With much of our deflated self-esteem, our wounded feelings, we don't want to be adjectives. Remember, pride is not based on an evil. A vice is simply a virtue gone mad. It's based on a very legitimate self-esteem that is not only legitimate but also commendable, and which should be an invaluable aid in doing good. We should esteem ourselves as children of God and not deface that image. We should love ourselves without being guilty of self-love. We should consider ourselves above the vicious and the vulgar, or even the second best.

Like most things it's a question of balance. There are times in life when we must pray simply: "O Lord, be merciful to me, a sinner"; and times when we can say with Mary of the *Magnificat*, "He who is mighty hath done great things to me." But let us be smart enough, dear friends, to know the difference.

# Civility

*J*AMES Reston recently observed that if one watches the news these days one can hardly avoid the impression that the United States is a nation of selfish factions, lobbies, and special-interest groups which have lost concern for the national interest, and have even lost the tradition of public and private civility. Financial crises, wildcat strikes, bribery, welfare cheating, sloppiness of service, commercial, professional, and political hostility — all these and more suggest we have lost our sense of the common good, and are breaking down into factional classes conducive to religious, economic, and racial strife.

With the rise of naturalistic philosophies, counterpointed by the decline of our religious traditions, we thought we could fashion a brave new world through science and politics. Religion along with its dynamism in our modern culture was thought a mere remnant of an obscurantist past. But those surrogate faiths have not worked out too well.

Science has shown that it can cure or kill with awesome brilliance, but it can't tell us which of the two we are to do. Science, as Bertrand Russell once said, is ethically neutral.

Politics effected a kind of unity when good and evil were supposedly embodied by good and bad nations. But politics has not only *not* succeeded in eradicating the hatred that divides nations, it also has not given us as a nation a public philosophy capable of operating society. We have neither an awareness of the past nor expectation of the future. We're a nation of "now" children, each of whom is fiercely engaged in defending his sphere of interest, and is rude to anyone who treads on his territory.

Obviously, we're not going to save our fragmented society by the invention of a new gadget or the fashioning of a new political gimmick. Our forefathers succeeded not because they were supermen but because they acted on principled intelligence. They were not always right, nor were they always good; but they realized that morality and principle must support civic and even domestic enterprises if we are to succeed.

Courtesy and civility are the outer ramparts of morality. And of course every faith is lived in a time and a place. We're inevitably creatures of our environment, and our environment is urban and largely industrialized — and our love of neighbor will make demands on us in terms of that kind of world.

Now, if charity is loving concern for self and for others, then it involves much more than desiring our neighbor's spiritual welfare, more even than helping him in time of great distress. Charity itself demands courtesy and civility. So when I say that these are the outer ramparts of morality and the loving concern that we call charity, I'm simply recognizing something much more.

Our age seems to be an age of rudeness. To hear a child use expressions like "Please," "Excuse me," and "Thank you" seems to be an increasingly rare experience. Now, I'm not merely talking about New York cabdrivers but about all of us. For years I've been going up to the National Tennis Championships, and I was recently at Flushing Meadow. It's appalling to see in our front ranks so many brilliant young crybabies. There seem to be so many raw talents unsurrounded by a person. And it's not just the hardened campaigners who have built up their dreary if limited vocabularies, but even the young teenage girls who come fortified with magnificent backhands and the vocabularies of fishwives.

One talented young lady was shocked that her opponent was shocked, as if a complaint about obscenity should be considered on the same level as a pleasantry about the weather. Another feisty young warrior was concerned not about the propriety of his language but about the propriety of somebody's listening to it.

Why are we so rude to one another? Do we think we're some kind of privileged species? "The ugly American" is an unfortunate expression. In the original work, of course, the ugly American was a very fine character; but the expression has come to signify the species of American for whom foreign culture, plumbing, and food are abominations. We do tend, I think, to exaggerate borders and nationalities too much. The astronauts never saw borders as they look out at that world in the distant blue. Perhaps we have so accepted the competitive American business ethic into the totality of our lives that "the other" is in some vague way our enemy or our opponent.

Perhaps we have accepted Hobbes's definition of combative man as a fundamentally hostile creature. Perhaps we have shrugged and said that that's the way it is in a dog-eat-dog world. But here we are faced with the counter-evaluation that our faith demands of us. Hostility, enmity, rudeness — this is simply not Christ's way. And if we choose to follow him, then his loving concern for the feelings and sensibilities of others will influence our lives significantly. We will see civility quite simply demanded by our Christian vocation.

A few years ago, love figured in the rhetoric of the cultural revolution; and yet we saw amazing insensitivity shown by the supposed love generation. In an amazing display of self-righteousness, the radical conscience picked saints and villains, and of course the villains were always the other person. Courtesy was scorned as an establishment hypocrisy; manners nothing more than a codification of such hypocrisy.

Now, these people were pompous bores more than anything else, but I think a New Testament faith *does* demand courtesy and civility as an intrinsic part of loving concern. It doesn't demand that we cannot strongly support a principle or strongly oppose an evil. Civility is not an escape of the weak but a virtue of the strong. It makes the associative character of social life not only endurable but possible. It fights against the selfish: our selfish selves. And there's never a time when we in some sense are not the enemy. Vices in others don't become virtues in us.

Let us ask the compassionate and kindly Christ for the perfection of charity that the years we live may be gracious years, perfectly compatible with strength of principle and strength of utterance but lived with a charity and civility that will give character, substance, and joy to our lives.

# Freedom

*T*HERE are fashions in thought as there are fashions in clothes. The spirit of our times is very distinctive, and one of the prominent characteristics of that spirit is a new attitude to freedom and responsibility.

In every sphere of life, permissiveness and a freer lifestyle are in the air. We notice this in the family, in the school and university, in our clubs, trades, and professions. All of these institutions reflect the mood, and we must face the fact that the Ten Commandments and the Creed (with their specific commitments and their specific prohibitions) often run counter to this spirit.

One free spirit has suggested that we shouldn't even talk about the Ten Commandments but instead should refer to them as the Ten Suggestions, lest we exacerbate the delicate sensibilities of contemporary man! Now, our

Blessed Lord doesn't force anybody to follow him, but he is explicit. The Church has doors that open in and out, and religion eventually will not be that which we inherit but that which we choose.

Saint Augustine once said, in a somewhat misunderstood phrase: "Love God and do what you will." Of course that is not a carte blanche permission to do anything you feel like; but if you really love God, the loving of God will be manifested in the way you live and not only in the way you think. And if you truly love God, you won't offend him. I think, however, in our society we have invented many caricatures for freedom. That's the idea to do anything, anytime, anywhere. That type of license has never really existed, and never could in any civilized society. It's a rather infantile notion of freedom.

Justice Holmes gave a classic formulation to this objection when he said that nobody is free to yell "fire" in a crowded theater. In other words, you're not suppressing the entrepreneurial spirit — supposedly indigenous in American society — if you prevent somebody from selling cocaine outside a junior high school.

Freedom is indeed necessary for the human spirit, but we're not interested in letting anybody do anything he wants, anytime, anywhere. We're interested, of course, in preventing arbitrary limitations of freedom. Freedom is necessary for the human spirit, and the drab tyrannies that have tried to enslave bodies and souls — and are still doing so — have never really succeeded (despite the agony they have caused through history). But freedom must mean more than mere liberation. It must involve a positive affirmation, the assumption of responsibility — and from that we cannot run.

What has happened in our society is that we have often thrown away rules, constraints, conventions, and courtesies; and rather than being truly liberated, we have become slaves to as many masters as we have appetites and inclinations. We've become slaves to whims. We have become escapees to a drug subculture or a subculture of promiscuity, free to use people as we use water fountains, free to abandon that self-discipline without which any effort — from marriage to business to athletics — must be eventually based.

Being free is not copping out. Every freedom has its commensurate responsibility, and if we want the one, we must have the other — if our freedom is to be truly creative. Another thing: We can't be mere observers of the human spectacle — we must be participants. The French have an expression, to be *au delà de la mêlée* — that is, to be outside the fight, watching from afar.

One of the saddest episodes in our recent history was that widely publicized Kitty Genovese story, when a young woman was murdered in New York, in full view of many people, none of whom bothered even to call the police because they didn't want to get involved. But we *are* involved. That's what Christ tells us week after week in the Gospel. And in Genesis we read, "Am I my brother's keeper?" That wasn't a rhetorical question. We *are* our brother's keeper; and his anguish, and his need, to some extent, must be ours. And his need limits my freedom. And when we help the halt and the lame, and the poor and the blind and the despairing, we are — if we are true Christians — helping Christ himself.

Remember that question in the New Testament, "When did I see thee, Lord?" Let us see today that being a Christian means being free, but that being free means more than absence from restraint; it means assuming the responsibility that our role in life would seem to suggest. This is my life and my world, and I can't blame the politician or the criminal if I don't do my part in making it a better world.

The civilized man is a disciplined man who knows that the glorious freedom of the children of God is the joy of the genuinely free who have used their liberty for the flowering of self and the redemption of their world. B.F. Skinner tells us that man is no more responsible for talking in church than he is for coughing in church. Now, it's this kind of learned nonsense that has encouraged contemporary evasion of responsibility, either by denying its existence or seeing guilt conveniently in the other fellow.

The associative life demands more than freedom to do. Your freedom ends where my nose begins, and if we are to build together, live together, create together, our individual freedoms must be tempered by intelligent restraint. No person, family, or society can survive without this sense of responsibility, and if our Lord tells us to learn of him, he presumes that we are free to choose to learn of him and that we really want to.

We must stop this abdication of a sense of personal responsibility. We must stop blaming our stars, our politicians, our unconscious drives. We should acknowledge that we are just as responsible for our sins, our injustices, and our failures as we are for the little triumphs for which we are never loath to claim credit. We can't have it both ways. We can't take refuge in determinism when we are evil, and move to stage front center for a bow when we are good. We can't wear ribbons of the hero when we are brave, unless we wear the sackcloth and ashes of the penitent when we are evil.

Freedom is indeed the meaning of our life and the meaning of our world, as Nikolai Berdyaev has suggested. But if we interpret liberty in a narrow political sense as freedom from foreign enemies; if a supposed increase in self-knowledge means an increase in moral paralysis; if we are victims rather than agents in the personal and social problems of our world — then we have already yielded to the enemy within our gates.

It was once thought that the cry of Lucifer, "I will not serve," was the most tragic of utterances; but it's more tragic when man thinks himself incapable of either service or defiance. At that hour I think our flight from freedom will be complete, and we shall have lost self as well as the battle.

There is a sentence in Christopher Fry's *The Lady's Not for Burning* which emphasizes this sense of responsibility. Fry says, "It is the individual man in his individual freedom who will, with the warmth of his spirit, mature the unripe world."

# Fidelity

$S$*AINT*

Paul in his Epistles, particularly in his Epistle to Timothy, tells us that we must remain faithful to what we have learned and believed. We must stay with a task, whether convenient or inconvenient, never losing patience.

It's really a plea for permanence in an age of impermanence. This letter was probably written by Saint Paul in A.D. 66 or 67 while he was a prisoner in Rome for the second and last time. Paul is alone. He is isolated. He knows that death awaits him. He sounds like a modern-day Kolbe or a Bonhoeffer in prison, because the true apostle, remember, is concerned about the message, not the messenger.

Paul doesn't wallow in self-pity. Rather, he's interested in the stability of the Christian community, the vitality of the faith, and the fidelity of the flock. How little the problems of faith change over the years.

Here is the greatest apostle of Christianity. His whole mission seems to be fruitless. He sees his isolation; he is brought to his knees. But for him it is the faith that counts, not his sensibilities, not his sense of personal fulfillment, and certainly not worldly judgments of success. His is the generous, the loyal, and the dedicated faith. He has served God as best he can, realizing that the moral life, like politics, is the art of the possible. Paul exhorts Timothy, in turn, to remain faithful, and never to lose patience — and he knows Timothy will keep the faith.

How often we hear the same lamentations today that we read about in Sacred Scripture. There are those who consider the Church imprisoned, beleaguered, ineffectual, out of date. They talk of our day as mankind come-of-age, free of the obscurantism and ignorance of a benighted past. They are smugly censorious of tradition, stability, and belief, equating promiscuity with self-fulfillment, indulgence with self-realization, and a lack of permanent commitment with liberty.

In the last century there were those who actually wanted to close the patent office because they felt that everything had been invented that could be invented. This is the egocentric illusion in its most egregious form. Of course the performance of Christians in the world has been poor. But is it not strange that in a world that does not expect perfection in its presidents, stockbrokers, quarterbacks, or cooks, people are ready to leave the Church because its performance is not perfect, because sermons are not eloquent, and bishops are not prophetic, because the effortlessly simple answer cannot be provided, or again, because it can? Infidelity in our age has become chic in a most radical way. Abandonment of religion and moral values is a supposed purer stance of an unfettered soul.

Infidelity, I would like to suggest, is rationalized delinquency — a hypocritical lack of principled behavior in the name of liberation. Those who leave the Church are now called "hidden" Catholics. I should like to suggest that they are painfully apparent secularists. We say that faith is alien to human experience, and then we climb into a box of steel and aluminum propelled by a small ocean of highly flammable fuel and flown by a pilot we have never seen, some five to seven miles above the earth. Faith alien to human experience?

We have faith in pharmacists and ushers, bus drivers and pilots. As a matter of fact, when we talk in terms of the unfaithful — those who have left the Church — I've known people who have left the Church for many

34

reasons; but strangely enough, I never knew of anybody that ever left the Church because he or she wanted to lead a better life. And I think in many cases, despite the rationalizations we hear, outside of the Church those who leave seem to become less and less Christian.

There is still that ancient question of Saint Peter's when Christ asked the disciples if they too would leave: "Lord, to whom shall we go?" Christ still speaks to us through the Church, however bad the sermon, however uninspiring or trivial the liturgy, however shortsighted the leadership. Neither Christian life nor Christian virtue is a species of entertainment, and neither is life. The grace and strength of Christ invigorate us still through his sacraments, his word, his life. The Word still nourishes; the Eucharist can still strengthen us in our weakness; the commandments of God can still guide us in our behavior; and prayer, however short and however informal, can still preserve an awareness of God's presence — and help us achieve quiet strength and balance, comfort in grief, and strength and courage in performance.

Saint Paul has another phrase, another admonition, that our uptight generation could well profit from: "Have patience." The young have a tendency to think that our problems are not solved only because of somebody's ignorance, malice, or laziness. Sometimes, of course, they're not solved because of the very enormity of the problems themselves. It would, of course, be nice and comforting to think that for every problem there is a readily available answer that comes with calculator swiftness and accuracy. We must find that happy medium between naïve expectation and paralyzing inactivity born of the belief that nothing can be done.

We do the best we can, when we can, with what we can — and we try to be patient with our world, patient with one another, and patient with ourselves. A television program may be able to wrap up life's problems in an hour or two, but life may not be that accommodating. We have to hold fast to the faith, realizing, of course, that everything about our culture is not conducive to holding fast to the Catholic faith at all.

In our society, the liberal has an abiding passion for making public confessions of other people's sins. We should rather be willing to confess our own sins without ceasing to try to have no sins to confess. But we probably won't ever be completely successful, and if we are patient with ourselves, we won't expect to be. Saint Paul was not speaking only to the backsliders but also to the brittle idealists who give up the fight because the battle is not won in the first skirmish.

Let us listen to Paul as he speaks to us across the years, asking us to be confident in the faith. Let us keep in mind that our Lord Jesus Christ (whom we all follow) is still the way, the truth, and the life. If we grow in the knowledge and love of our Lord and Savior, all will indeed be well.

# Humor

## *G*. K.

Chesterton once said he thought that our Lord had one secret that the Twelve Apostles never revealed — a gentle sense of humor. Unfortunately, many people associate humor with frivolity, but I should like to suggest that a gentle sense of humor is one of the greatest shock absorbers in existence.

Saint Francis de Sales phrased it well when he said, "A saint who is sad is a sad sort of saint." Many people think that they are being serious merely because they are being solemn, and solemn people have been aptly described as people who habitually look at the serious side of things that have no serious side.

Now, I'm not for one moment making a plea for frivolity or an irresponsible lack of seriousness. The Latin missal, for instance, has a wonderful description of Saint Bruno, a little-known saint. His life is described as a life of serene gaiety. The grim apostle is a contradiction in terms — and so, of course, is the grim disciple.

The greatest truth of Christianity is that we are children of the Resurrection. We have been promised eternal life. We are children of a loving God. We have been told that the very hairs of our head are numbered, that our Father's solicitude will follow us all the days of our lives.

Now, if we truly believe that, how can we reflect cynicism and gloom and depression to our generation? Of course, sadness will come into our lives, but we're not expected to make sadness a way of life. If it is God's will that we bear a cross, then it should be our will too; but I think humor gives a certain ease to people and things and gives us strength for the long haul. I have met many of these grim, humorless people who feel that life is too serious for laughter. They become hard and brittle and, lacking resiliency, they are the first to crack in difficult situations — and the first to be disillusioned when their ideals are not quickly realized.

Louis Evely, in his little book *That Man Is You*, says: "It's not enough to put the brakes on if the motor is still whirring inside." The whirring of our solicitous selves should be attuned to a slower rhythm, and I think a gentle sense of humor is really linked to a kind of poverty of spirit. Notice, I say "gentle," for ridicule is cruelty, not humor.

But we have to start with ourselves, to laugh at our pretensions and posturing, to laugh at our fears, and even, at times, our mistakes — for the man who refuses to recognize humor in himself is usually a prideful person, as is the abnormally sensitive of whom all must be aware. The fact is that at one time or another we will make clowns of ourselves, and often laughter is the best cure. We should accept ourselves not only for what we can be but what we are; and laughing at the exalted image we sometimes have of self, we can go forward with greater ease.

Our lives must be based on an interior solidity and a flexibility to meet the crises that inevitably come. Grimness has never solved a thing — it only gives the false illusion of sobriety. The world has very little need of brittle enthusiasts. We need men like Saint Thomas More, a man for all seasons, who kept his sense of humor even on the scaffold itself when he said: "Pray for me, as I shall pray for thee, until we meet merrily in heaven." Or again, as he prepared to die: "I pray you, Master Lieutenant, see me safe up, and for my coming down, let me shift for myself."

# Special Moments

*O*NE
of the most unique experiences we have are those rather extraordinary moments, those very special moments of our lives that seem to be instants of great sensitivity and insight. Sometimes these insights may be triggered by a very simple thing. And they happen not only to an Archimedes, a Descartes, or a Newton — but to us all. Sometimes they are moments of joy. Sometimes they are moments of sadness, but somehow they seem to disclose to us more than the average experience. They reveal something about our world and also something about ourselves.

The New Testament's word for such a decisive moment is *kairos*, the Greek word for "the time of favor." I was thinking of such a moment not too long ago as I stood in Westminster Abbey in London before the throne of Saint Edward the Confessor, who died over nine hundred years ago, thinking of the stability and permanence of the faith, and how the past speaks to us.

We are not only a young nation as nations go, but even contemporary culture emphasizes the present at the expense of the past and future. We are "Now" people. We lock in on the world of now with blinders on, and it's an inadvertent intolerance of the past — even though, of course, intolerance is the last thing in the world the contemporary man would like to think himself guilty of.

I think we all need a sense of belonging as a source of strength and continuity. We are often a fragmented people, reacting from moment to moment without an underlying foundation, and we need integration. The foundation of our faith as Christians is adherence to a divine Christ, and this is the primary insight; but it should be reinforced by the examples of the saints through the centuries. Christ was their strength, and Christ was their joy — and if they seemed to be supermen, it was just that they had an extraordinary love of Christ that made everything endurable, and an extraordinary familiarity with adherence to Christ's way of life.

I think our faith should not be simply an insight derived from the great disclosure moments of death and life but a progressive series of insights into ourselves and our world and its people, something that we increase by grace, especially through the Eucharist.

Happiness is not something that is frantically pursued; it's something we become as we realize that we as Christians are Christ's family in a very real sense, and that our ties extend both to the past and to the future. That is why, for instance, prayer should be an important part of the daily spiritual life of the Christian. It helps us to see and to understand. It doesn't insulate us from life; it doesn't make us selfishly oblivious of the world's pain; instead it gives us a power to see things in perspective, and act accordingly.

When Christ said to his disciples, "Let not your hearts be troubled," it wasn't because he was going to shield them from life, or anesthetize them to the frightful situations that they would shortly be facing. Their inner power would prove to be stronger than anything the world of materialists could bring against them, and even stronger than other competing ideas. The throne of Edward the Confessor is a symbol of power, but it suggests faith and continuity. It is obviously a very old chair to the casual observer; but it stands for something far more significant than its decaying pieces, for the idea will always be more powerful than the thing. Things are locked in their own isolated materiality, and that's why things alone can't satisfy the aspirations of the human heart. But an idea can soar and can encompass; it lives. The faith of an Edward the Confessor is our faith, and it speaks to us across the centuries and it should give shape and meaning and significance to all that we have and all that we do.

Let us forget the positivist illusion that equates the real with that which we can taste and touch and see and feel. That is a kind of limited vision — and narrow-mindedness of the worst sort. We continue to follow the fortunes of a young Church. Let us ask in our prayer for the enrichment, both of vision and decision, that our faith be a realization of our past, and a light into the future.

# Discouragement

*T*HE theme of discouragement often is referred to in the liturgy. It is hardly a new phenomenon; but I think it's a particular problem of our time because our society has in a special way repudiated tradition and its stabilities, having embraced the now and its real and illusory possibilities.

The reasons might be said to be cultural, psychological, and religious. It is an attitude that has been more formally phrased as an existentialist one, an attitude of mind committed to modernity, self, and emancipation, rather than to conformity and tradition. It involves suspicion of tradition, custom, structure, and institution, whether it be ecclesiastical, social, or civil.

But when there is a reliance on the traditional, there is certain stability and strength that the past provides, though there is the danger that it will harden into intransigence. Peter Drucker has spoken of the erosion of continuities in our society. Home, church, and government cannot claim the allegiance they once did.

It's an interesting statistic that in the frightful increase of suicides among our youth in the last decade, the least inclined to kill themselves are those who live in structured homes — even if the discipline there is too strict or even unreasonable. All of this is part of the cultural background of discouragement. To be liberated means not only to be emancipated from bonds but also to be bereft of support. I'm not saying we should divinize tradition; we should rather balance the principle of tradition which recognizes what is enduring in the past with a principle of innovation which recognizes what is promising in the future.

The unhappy fact is that there is an appalling amount of unhappiness and discouragement in our permissive society, and there is an appalling amount of discouragement in those reasonably affuent, and suffering none of the frightful deprivations of the boat people or those starving to death in the Sahel south of the Sahara in Africa. There is a great prevalence of alienation and discouragement that beclouds lives, dissipates love, and paralyzes effort. And in this segment of society it is often not the obvious problems of the poor, the sick, the aged, and the hungry. We know why they are discouraged. They have plenty to be discouraged about. But many lives have the problem of sheer emptiness: lives devoid of principle, religion, loyalties to people or institutions; lives unwarmed by affection or enthusiasm, or even tepid interest. Saint Paul, of course, complained how dull and flat, stale and unprofitable, the things of earth were; but he had a compensating faith.

Emptiness should be replaced by affirmation because life quite simply needs affirmation — not blind faith but initially a recognition, an intellectual curiosity that reflects the fact that there are some values worth affirming. Our faith, our good sense, and our reasonable expectation — all of these should help us cope successfully with the disappointments of life. Christ tells us we should take up our crosses daily, that our rewards will be a hundredfold in eternal life. Christian hope should dissipate gloom and discouragement if our faith is real.

And what I'm saying essentially is not that our society does not give reason for anxiety and discouragement but that we are more discouraged than perhaps we should be; and this is not a condition with which we are inevitably saddled, given minimum conditions of physical and psychological health. We simply should not buy the spurious values of contemporary culture that amount to an anarchic independence, which promises so much and delivers so little.

Psychologically, we should tailor expectations to the real world and recognize the degree to which our talent, courage, and industry justify our expectations. And, spiritually, we should realize that suffering is not a repudiation of life but a dimension of it. We can indeed learn sympathy and compassion for others, and above all we can remember that despite our griefs over things real or imagined, we are still destined to be children of joy. Perhaps if we were less preoccupied with the self and its problems as William James suggested, and occupied ourselves with the more obvious needs of our fellows, our cares — like autumn leaves — would be deciduous, and our self-pity unnecessary.

# Forgiveness

*T*HE theme of forgiveness is one that our Lord emphasizes again and again in the New Testament.

Perhaps one of the few things we remember in the New Testament is, "Go thou first and be reconciled to thy brother." It's one of charity's most difficult exercises and perhaps one of the most indispensable. Whether our Lord is talking of the wicked servant or the prodigal son, or in the imagery of finding the silver piece that was lost, he indicates that God is not only a just judge but a loving father.

He assumes human frailty without condoning its excesses, and tells us quite simply that a disciple of his must do the same. Now, of course, we don't have any difficulty with the first part — receiving forgiveness for *our* trespasses; but when we are asked to forgive the frailty of our brother, *his* evil, *his* neglect, *his* inconsiderateness — that's a different matter. We clutch our hurts to our bosoms as if the injuries were precious possessions and we don't really want to let go.

Sin, like death, we can always somehow tolerate because we associate it with somebody else — not that our Lord is asking us to be wishy-washy indifferentists, unable or unwilling to distinguish between right and wrong. He is adamant in condemning the sin but not the sinner. "Go and sin no more," our Lord tells us.

It's comforting to picture the New Testament problems as exclusively concerned with the obdurate hearts of a far-off time in a far-off place. That is the comforting illusion of remoteness: *those* sins and *those* people. This, of course, is both the fallacy of distance and the fallacy of time. But we really know in our hearts that through the Gospels our Lord is telling us here and now to be compassionate and forgiving human beings, even while espousing the principled life. He assumes that we might indeed have been grievously wronged and imposed upon. A grudge, you know, can be very heavy baggage to carry, and it is simply not Christ's way.

Our charity often becomes selective over the years. It seems that we want only to love the lovable. Our forgiveness is sometimes counterfeited by an icy condescension that is neither love nor warmth, nor compassionate understanding. You know it's odd too, because what is understandable in ourselves becomes incomprehensible in others. Even in our wildest flights of self-delusion we admit to faults. We expect to be forgiven, but we are not always ready to forgive or to forget. There's that famous phrase, of course: "I can forgive but I can't forget," which is another way of saying that I haven't really forgiven.

Take individual family members, neighbors, business associates, and friends from whom we've become estranged for one or both of these reasons: First, they perhaps behaved abominably, which is regrettable but understandable, since they are human; and second, they simply don't meet our expectations for the most trivial and frivolous of reasons.

Of course we will be deeply hurt sometimes in life, even by loved ones, but that's part of the human experience. Look at even the tremendous psychological differences between husband and wife in the closest of unions. When he is needed most, perhaps he becomes the obtuse and insensitive male, unaware but not malicious. Perhaps she is oblivious of a triumph he considers really important. Sometimes friends are not there when we need them most; sometimes they seem to be blind to our needs. It's almost as if God wants us to be alone, as he was alone in Gethsemane.

There's a danger here too of drowning in a sea of self-pity. I always think of one of Thomas Wolfe's characters, Eliza Gant, in *Look Homeward, Angel*. She wallows in self-pity and plays the martyr. Her drunken husband seems to be almost a kind of prized possession. It is perhaps an unkind suspicion — even of the fictitious Eliza — but I wonder if his improbable sobriety would really have been a blessing. Eliza might have lost the martyr's crown.

Let's take another lesson from the Lord — not in how we treat our enemies but how we treat those we love. Let's work harder at this whole business of being compassionate, forgiving human beings. You know, playing God is very difficult when one is not God. And it's been said that once we find out how to be authentically human, we won't want to play God. We can't be handsome or beautiful or witty or sparkling or brilliant, but we can be more humanly human. I remember the phrase of Teilhard de Chardin: "I wish to become conscious of all that the world loves, pursues, and suffers. I want to be the first to seek, sympathize and to suffer. The first to unfold and sacrifice myself, to become more widely human, and more nobly of the earth than any of the world's servants."

The idea of forgiving others suggests also the question: Are we only to forgive and tolerate carbon copies of ourselves? The biggest pain in society — and there are as many aspirants for this dubious honor as there are people — is the sensitive person always looking for slights. He mistakes pride for elegance, and selfishness for virtue. You know, I think the uncharitableness and rigidity of the so-called good people (whom Bernanos called "the devout") is a scandal to behold. It's often the vice of the respectable who may call themselves sinners in their prayers but don't really expect to be believed, even by God.

We're rather uneasy these days with the whole notion of sin, and we tend to consider transgressions tolerated eccentricities except when they're the tabloid vices. We think vice is only vice when it's vulgar or palpably obscene. Sometimes I think that if our middle-class Christians ever had to vote on the readmission of the prodigal son, he probably would still be living off the husks of swine. Why? Because we all picture ourselves as the elder brother when we should be classifying ourselves perhaps as the prodigal son. We often resemble the dear lady who, upon hearing the Gospel of the Pharisee and the publican, said: "Thank God I'm like the publican."

We don't really have to be Charles Mansons to be evil. In a sense we're all prodigal sons, forgiven again and again by an indulgent Father. Our Lord is being definitive here, for our soul's salvation depends on a living charity, not a haughty, personalized propriety that we have relabeled virtue. In the course of a lifetime we all will be hurt, slighted, ignored, or insulted; but we Christians cannot afford to be estranged. That is part of the *human* experience. But to be hurt and to forgive — that is part of the *Christian* experience.

# Weariness

*O*NE

of the maladies of the twentieth century seems to be the malady of weariness. One of the expressions heard very often is "burn out," which seems to mean sheer fatigue rather than acute suffering. We read in the Sacred Scriptures, "Come to me all you who are weary and find life burdensome, and I shall refresh you." If we take our yoke upon our shoulders, if we learn of him, our souls will find rest.

Now, this is a rather remarkable guarantee made by our Lord, and we might ask ourselves, "Do we really believe it?" Do we really believe that the Christ whom we follow will give us rest and peace when life is wearisome or burdensome? Or do we dissociate our faith from our problems unless we find ourselves in situations of desperation and pray when all else fails? The formal title was semi-Pelagian, a last-gasp dependence; but the idea is that prayer is kind of a fire-insurance policy in case your own efforts fail. There's an old Indian proverb that says: "Pray to God, but row away from the rocks." In short, despite our pretensions of faith, do we (on the one hand) look upon our faith as something "in here," in the Church — and real life (on the other hand) as something "out there," in the marketplace? Our two lives are like lines that never seem to intersect. Our prayer life and our spiritual considerations are somehow part of a second, nebulous world, alien to normal concerns of daily life.

Is the Catholic faith a ceremonial stamp we put on baptisms, weddings, and funerals, or is it a living thing within us, whose strength we bring to daily situations and events? We are not meant to be believers only when all else fails. Why not be believers throughout the day, throughout our lives? Christ is not "there" only when we are fearful disciples walking on the water and holding out our hands to him in desperation or terror. He tells us, rather, that he is our quiet companion of the voyage. He tells us he will be with us all days, even to the consummation of the world, and our lives are meant to be lived in quiet and serene confidence, despite external turmoil.

Of course life will sometimes break our hearts, but even grief should not be the desperation so widespread in our society. We really wouldn't want to be sequestered from life, isolated from the exultation or sorrow of our world. But if we neglect our prayer (especially if we neglect the Eucharist), if we neglect our reading of the Word of God, the faith — though it may not be formally rejected — can indeed become increasingly remote, an untapped resource in our lives.

If we Christians seem at times to react like secularists, may it not be because we have become more secularistic than Christian? It's appalling to consider how much desperation there is in our world. The Golden Gate Bridge alone in San Francisco has been the scene of more than six hundred suicides. How much anguish did the poor people take with them!

And look at the surrogate gods that we have invented to ease the pain. They range all the way from astrology to indulgence. The best-seller lists feature the books that tell us how to be number one, no matter who else gets bruised or stepped on. Sexual license is represented as fulfillment. Wealth is fulfillment. Selfishness is fulfillment. The fad of the month is fulfillment. And the bizarre cults are fulfillment.

But the libertines of the human family have always been among the most miserable. And affluence, though it solves many problems, creates others — and often leaves the successful and the affluent curiously unhappy and searching. We have rejected Christ and divinized the folk heroes, who are usually more mixed-up than anybody else.

In our spiritless little world we are like Pagliaccis trying to find someone to make us laugh. Christ is not gone. He's never been away. And he still says to us quietly: "Your souls will find rest." Not in extinction or in feverish distraction, nor in an insensitive private Nirvana of indifference, nor in avid pursuit of the pleasure of the moment. He is still the way, the truth, and the life — and the only thing that can keep him and the richness of his promise to us away from us is our indulgent and negligent selves.

We should in our prayer accept the invitation of the Christ who promises us the strength and the grace and the serenity to live our lives with joy, and to provide rest for that weariness which seems to be so much a part of the human condition.

# Belonging

*T*HE liturgy sometimes speaks of our promised inheritance, "Our sonship in Christ," "The chosen flock," "The bond of a common faith in Christ."

In short, it's all about belonging. It's often been observed that life's happiness is not so much of a "getting" as a "finding": finding something big enough to give ourselves to — a worthy object of our love and loyalty; a focal point of our interests; the inspiration of our striving. We often think that the first disciples were supermen or superwomen to have challenged with such courage the civil and religious establishments of their day. By the fallacy of distance we think of them as larger than life.

They weren't, really. They were as impulsive as Peter, as avaricious as Judas, and as sinful as Magdalene. They even had fond mothers trying to get them privileged places in Christ's kingdom. They doubted like Thomas. In short, they were quite human, very much like us in our human frailty, exhibiting at times the foibles and at times the greatness of the human condition.

But they had the great strength of a shared faith. They belonged, and they knew they belonged. They were a little flock; but they were Christ's little flock, and the terror of persecution and the blandishments of their world could not disturb that depth and that serenity — a fact which dismayed even their enemies.

We have observed that this sense of belonging — or more properly, the need to belong — has enticed many of the rootless and alienated into bizarre and often destructive cults. Even those who speak the language of liberation and permissiveness need a center, a spiritual self, to make the fragments of reality hang together. The great French skeptic Voltaire once said that if there were no God, men would have to create one.

Christ's disciples were indeed strong, as we can be strong if we grow in faith — if, instead of playing the game of Sunday Christians, we are really the living flock of Jesus Christ. If we nourish ourselves in the Eucharist, if we read his words daily, if we bring back prayer into our activist lives — then we too can grow and have an increasing psychological sense of belonging to the strength which is Christ.

Some time ago the comic Richard Pryor, who is usually more concerned with scatology than eschatology, said: "Using drugs is the greatest feeling in the world, unless you want to be a human being." Drug use is another spurious answer to the question of life. One asks: "How do I live? What gives my life meaning? How can I face suffering? To whom do I really belong?"

People don't alter their vision of reality, unless they are unhappy with the vision they have — and drug use is *not* better living through chemistry. We cannot find that center of life in bizarre experimentation. We won't find it in drugs or promiscuity, or in the amassing of material things, because we are not merely things. And even when we find oblivion in something like alcohol, we always have to awake from temporary oblivion, because sensation is not love, faddism is not faith, and happiness is not glandular. We still have to work at being members of the little flock. Christ is still there with his strength, his grace, and his joy to answer the need for belonging that exists in the human heart. And we have the same human equipment the saints had. The Gospels, remember, are not mere histories of far-off saints in far-off struggles in a far-off time. The Gospels demand a resonance in our lives here and now. It is a joy to realize what belonging to Christ really means. We are not alone. We are not forgotten. We are his people.

# Ambiguity

$I_N$
the musical comedy *The King and I*, the king of Siam (now Thailand), as played by Yul Brynner, perplexed by a combination of responsibility and moral ambiguity, expresses his doubt in a song that he sings in rather quaint English: "Is a puzzlement!" And I suppose that as we reflect on the perplexities of contemporary life, and the ambiguities we perceive, we are tempted at times to say, "Is a puzzlement!"

How do we cope with a world whose values and practices seem so dramatically different from the world we knew and the world that Christ envisioned? How do we communicate effectively with our young, whose lives are not buttressed either by old certainties or new enthusiasms? Their conduct often is not guided by traditional truth of Church or family. How do we reconcile the demands of an aggressive, competitive society with the counsels of the Gospels? How can we not help but feel that our Lord's kind of Christian cannot survive in the kind of world in which we must live and work? How can we keep forgiving those who have betrayed our trust, taken advantage of our friendship, violated our rights, or injured our persons? It's a puzzlement!

But perhaps the puzzlement is not an unanswerable one. Perhaps we expect to be sheltered and advised and too much protected. Perhaps we have not perceived that in the providence of God, despite general guidance on

54

basic truths, we must make character-building choices. We must, in a certain sense, make up in ourselves those things that are wanting in the suffering of Christ. We must reason and we must choose, not out of obvious self-interest but by applying Christ's general value system to the specifics of our lives.

The French writer Albert Camus once said, "I am the sum of my choices." We should tailor our expectations and we should learn to live with ambiguity without using it as a shield to hide behind. We are, in the last analysis, the architects of our own lives. Quite simply, we won't find in the New Testament all the answers to the problems of living. But we certainly can point ourselves in the right direction. We do have the Apostles' Creed. We do have the Church's teaching magisterium. We do have the counsels of the Sermon on the Mount. We can be fortified by grace and the strength of the sacraments, confidently hopeful of being inspired by the Holy Spirit and guided by a Christ-established Church. A daily reading of the New Testament can recall to us our Lord's reaction to situations and people and events — and help us do the same. But it's not a complete catalog of answers and was never meant to be. God has given us the awesome power of free choice and we must have the courage and the goodness to move at times into an uncharted future with faith and good will.

Other cultures in other times were perhaps more paternalistic, but in God's providence we can apply principles to situations. I think in other times (as in our own immigrant past) the Church provided perhaps too much shelter. Sometimes the Church's pastors were too quick to give answers in purely secular matters in which clerics had no particular expertise. Of course there will sometimes be profound implications of a moral nature in secular concerns; but I think the Holy Father has been wise in his visits to Mexico, Brazil, and the Philippines to counsel restraint in purely political involvement by churchmen. Where is that line between legitimate concern in moral questions and political involvement? It's a good example of the ambiguity of which I speak. Sometimes we quite simply do not know the answer, but we have to try to find it. Saint Paul once used what at first seemed to be a peculiar expression that I've already quoted, "I make up in myself those things that are wanting in the suffering of Christ."

Wanting? Surely Christ's redemptive power is complete. Surely God doesn't need man. Of course Christ's redemptive power is complete. Of course God doesn't need us, but he chooses to make us a part of our own redemption. He chooses to give us the power to evaluate and decide and to share in his suffering. We've got the responsibility whether we like it or not; but, remember, we are also destined to share in his eternal joy.

Ambiguity is not doubt, and certainty is not always a guarantee.

# The Unholy Trinity

*T*HE

Christian life seems progressively anachronistic, preaching as it does prayer and asceticism in an age of gratification and pleasuring. I was reminded of this when I recently saw an advertisement of a contemporary television film, one of the most forgettable of recent vintage, called *The Betsy*. It's about the unholy trinity of sex, power, and money. Harold Robbins, the author, a writer whose style has been described as glandular rather than literary, has explored this theme in a manner that is often witless, tasteless, and endless. But he has captured the popular mood. He exploits what has been called the eroticization of the social backdrop. Only a sociologist could coin a term like that.

Power and money, of course, have always been minor divinities in our society. Now, even if we don't intend to run to the nearest drugstore or go to the deathless prose of Harold Robbins, frail humans do find it easy to misplace the right ordering of power, affection, and possession in their lives. We can be entrapped by the things we have as much as we can be distressed by the things we don't have. Avarice erodes the ability to enjoy what we do have, and it seems also to deliver a strangely sullen dissatisfaction with "quantity of things" posing as "quality of life." We have assumed acquisition to be the answer; but there is a point at which acquisition becomes tedium and disenchantment — a point at which things use us, and then they are no longer at our service.

The asceticism that counsels moderation and restraint in the use of things is naturally as well as supernaturally desirable. Power too is a heady wine. For instance, each political regime that comes to power brings in its own team, a team made up of people who give the impression that power is going to last forever; and in a few years they are forgotten figures, leaving on an inauguration day for home — and sometimes jail. But while they have power, how faithfully they work from morning to night to the detriment of family and all else. Why are we so ardent in the worship of surrogate gods, and so tepid and lukewarm in the service of God himself? I suppose it's because the rewards are so immediate and obvious, if only for a time, and our world has enshrined feeling over reflection.

As for money (which we equate with success), both the rich man and the pauper have twenty-four hours in a day; and money can up to a point see that those twenty-four hours can be spent well. As one wag said it, "Money can't buy happiness, but it can allow you to be unhappy in comfort." Certainly an absence of money is almost a certain guarantee that those twenty-four hours can be spent miserably. We must achieve our salvation in the material conditions of our own society, not in some imaginary world of the future or historical world of the past. It is not money but the love of money that is described as the root of all evil. And it is not poverty but poverty of spirit that is described as a virtue. Poverty itself is a condition and not a virtue. A person may be poor simply because he is ineffectively avaricious. Poverty can degenerate into destitution, a grinding and debasing thing. And there is certainly nothing wrong with a legitimate solicitude for financial security in today's world. But sex, power, and money in *The Betsy* tradition are not going to provide the answer to the American dream.

I remember the story of a young farm boy riding a horse furiously past a group of his friends. (I think it was a story that was told by Stephen Leacock.) They yelled at the boy, "Where are you going in such a hurry?" And he yelled back, "I don't know! Ask the horse!" These idols are the horse, and we should ride the horse or the horse most assuredly will ride us.

# Complexity

*M*ANY

years ago, when I was first being introduced to the complexities of the Latin tongue, I learned something in Latin grammar called indirect discourse. Language is always fascinating, both as a means of expressing and concealing one's thoughts. As a student in Paris I remember being startled to hear street cleaners and garage mechanics speaking the fluent French that I had to work so hard to acquire, and I also remember being visited by an American acquaintance who felt if he repeated himself loudly enough in English that anyone not a congenital idiot should be able to understand him. I remember too sharing a railway carriage from Düsseldorf to Cologne with a seven-year-old German boy who could not quite understand how that older fellow to whom he was speaking seemed so hesitant and tentative in the speech in which he was so terrifyingly fluent.

But, of course, any language is but the agreed-upon symbol of the reality to anyone — that is, to anyone but a Frenchman. And I think the complexity of verbal discourse, a new kind of indirect discourse, reflects how we have tortured simple ideas into complexity as a means of avoiding responsibility. For instance, we talk about abortion in terms of the poor and in terms of women's rights, when the essential question is quite simply whether or not one ought to kill babies. We talk about personality realization and self-fulfillment, when what is involved is simply a question of fairness or justice, or whether or not one should honor solemn commitments. We call political prisoners thugs who blow up airplanes because they love humanity but hate people. What we call fanaticism in others is admirable principle in ourselves. You have hang-ups, I have convictions.

Now, I think some direct discourse is helpful to all of us, particularly when the penitential season of Lent is approaching. We are sinners, and we need — through prayer and mortification — the grace and strength to sin less. It has been said that a teacher's role is to render himself gracefully superfluous. Unfortunately, we never reach the point where self-discipline and prayer become superfluous. But the saints do show us what we can become, what priorities can become operative in our lives.

In the readings of Isaiah and Matthew for the Lenten liturgy we are told quite simply that we must share our bread with the hungry. The Massachusetts Institute of Technology's Dale Runge tells us it's unethical to feed the starving, because in the long run it will keep breeders alive who will compound the problem. Matthew, on the other hand, says, "You are the light of the world. Your light must shine before men that they may see goodness in your acts." Neither Isaiah nor our Lord tells us to feed the starving only if computer projections do not reveal demographic problems.

The man of faith has goals and reasonable self-knowledge. He has a mind to help him decide about priorities in life. He's not infallible; but he sees the obvious difference between murder and charity, cruelty and compassion, brutality and considerateness. He recognizes the factor of human frailty, and prayerfully seeks the grace to be what God can make of him. The man of faith does not seek salvation in exotic successive fads or quick solutions.

I remember once a rather whimsical piece that included this advice: "Never play poker with a man called Doc, and never eat in a restaurant called Mom's. You will be fleeced in the first and poisoned in the other." I'd like to add a third. Never buy a faith that dispenses with prayer and mortification in favor of wood-nymph blissfulness that entails no unpleasantness and no obligation. Never buy a philosophy of life that would destroy all guilt feelings, because the guilty *should* feel guilty. Happiness has been huckstered to our generation as consisting in everything from sexual athleticism to owning the "in" car or using the right deodorant. Let's uncomplicate our lives. Let's speak in rather direct discourse to see what we are and what we should do. We have in God our beginning and our end, and we have the time in between to fashion our lives for good or for ill. Let's make those days in between reflect in us the light that is Christ. Let us, in short, prepare more meaningfully to be Resurrection children.

# Courage

*D*URING

a recent holiday period I had the chance to reread the Dickens classic *David Copperfield*. The book over the years had lost none of its charm for me; but it did have a new message — the message of courage and its necessity if we would live happy lives.

Besides his dear Agnes, there were three great loves in David's life. First, there was his lovely but ineffectual mother; then there was his helpless child-bride, Dora; and finally, there was his brilliant but unstable friend Steerforth. He loved them all, but he complained that they were their own worst enemies because they wouldn't face life. They lacked courage. They lacked that staying power that would make possible any progress or any significant accomplishment.

He describes them as "the tinseled people who glisten for a while, and then fade away." He implies that by not sidestepping life their lives would have been meaningful and joyous. But not only were they failures, they also failed those who loved them.

I think the fictional David Copperfield can teach us something, because, after all, fictional characters are derived from life. We do need courage, courage to do the right thing when the wrong thing is the easy and the popular way out; courage to be faithful to principle, to family — even in the face of opposition or hostility; courage to endure in an impatient, nonpersevering age, realizing that suffering and difficulty are parts of life rather than its negation.

This is one of our age's greatest faults — a lack of perseverance and enduring patience, a lack of sustained will. We live in a television culture with its two-hour solutions — and all of life's problems are not that simple. But our here-and-now culture isn't prepared to hang in there.

We need courage to refuse to be overwhelmed by grief, illness, or adversity — though all three we shall know at some time in life. We need courage to try, to dare; we need courage to avoid paralysis in the name of prudence, spinelessness in the name of caution, and surrender in the name of diplomacy. Even Saint Paul, Christianity's greatest apostle, was very apprehensive in view of the enormity of his mission. But our Lord tells him as he tells us: "My grace is sufficient for thee." And Paul himself had to encourage Timothy, his young disciple, not to be ashamed of his testimony in behalf of the Lord.

We need courage in every situation; but courage is not foolhardiness because we as Resurrection children do have a divine guarantee, so to speak, of divine help. "I can do all things in him who strengthens me."

Courage or fortitude is listed among the gifts of the Holy Spirit, and like most virtues it admits of both excess and defect. A defective courage is cowardice, and often cowardice is not the abject cringing in dramatic situations, but selling out in quiet, almost unnoticed ways in order to be powerful, popular, successful, or wealthy.

Courage may be sinned against by excess, by irresponsible foolhardiness, foolish risk-taking. There often comes a time in the lives of both men and women when a quasi-panic comes — a vague feeling that life is passing them by; a feeling, perhaps, that all those great dreams of youth are not going to be realized, and a reluctance to settle for what seems to be a humdrum life.

One needs courage to go on at this particular juncture — courage perhaps to meet one's responsibilities and do the obligatory undramatic quiet things. So often in the past we have seen people in both lay and religious life rationalize delinquency and selfishness in the name of self-fulfillment. Those who admire this wood-nymph philosophy often ridicule those who are courageous enough to persevere.

Courage, indeed, has many faces, and in life we may have to ask our Lord for an increase of it. All of us would like in a crucial situation to exhibit grace under pressure. I have been impressed over the years especially with the courage of terminal patients from all walks of life. Almost invariably they do not consider themselves especially brave or courageous but feel that God gives them the grace and the strength — as he will give us the grace and the strength — to cope with what life brings. He has promised us this: that we can exhibit grace under pressure, because he will be our strength, and our courage, and, eventually, our life.

Robert Louis Stevenson had a lovely prayer on courage: "Give us grace and strength to forebear and to persevere. Give us courage and gaiety and the quiet mind."

# Anger

$S_{OME}$

time ago, I went to Grosse Pointe, Michigan, having been commanded to do so by a little girl (about to receive her first communion) whom I had previously baptized.

In the course of her theological speculations she asked me: "Was Jesus ever mad?"

In reflecting that our Lord vigorously condemned the Pharisees as whited sepulchers, and drove the money changers physically from the temple, I had to admit that our Lord — in the little girl's sense of the word — did get mad. I did this by way of answering the implied question that sometimes not mere indignation but anger is justified.

Our Lord was indeed righteously indignant over both hypocrisy and profanation; but my little friend's question set me to thinking about the possibility of fitting anger, in general, into a Christian framework. The Latin poet Horace once said: "Anger is a short madness." And I think Horace was close to the truth, because anger is often associated with grotesque overreaction. We have a memory of the fury provoked by the filling-station lines of a few years ago. We remember perhaps the scene in the film *Network*, in which people shout their wrath from apartment windows that "they're not going to take it anymore!"

Anger in contemporary culture seems to have become respectable, even worthy of praise. It is regularly mistaken for sincerity, which is today the ultimate virtue, whether or not it involves blowing up airplanes or feeding the poor. Of course it still depends on what we are sincere about. It is the accepted proof of moral conviction; so the madder we are, supposedly the purer is our dedication to an ideal. Melvin Maddocks, in an essay on anger, cites a modern parable of the absurd by Eugene Ionesco, in which a tranquil Sunday afternoon of a happy, peaceful town is shattered because husbands find flies in their soup. Smiles turn progressively into frowns, complaints, insults, fights, and then, absurdly, into war — all of this supposedly because of a fly in the soup.

It is, of course, a kind of dark humor. But it does indicate how close to the surface of civility the ugly emotion of anger — searing, withering anger — exists. I think one of the reasons why anger has become so acceptable in the contemporary scene is that it's part of our love of the spontaneous. It is, I believe, more correctly identified as a capital sin, despite the occasional lyricism with which it is frequently espoused by psychiatrists and clinical psychologists. We read: "Intimate hostilities should be programmed."

So in order to achieve some kind of personal catharsis and relief, we are encouraged to scatter the venom of our undisciplined selves in all directions. Of course people will be hurt, but we'll feel great.

This, dear friends, is another fatuity of our bright new world. It is nonsense. Anger can be an alarm system for our deepest concerns; but it can also be a form of undiscriminating, primitive violence of word and deed directed not only against enemies but against spouse and children.

Destructive violence in human relations can be culturally accentuated. Frustration and anger simply do not legitimize bashing in somebody's skull. A game of squash or a run around the block might satisfy those who feel the need for physical externalization of tension, although this need for externalization has its silly side too. Uncritically to consider anger a virtue and its unleashing an art form is crude self-indulgence.

The French philosopher Jean Jacques Rousseau, in his work *Emile*, once counseled: "Let him run, shout or fight whenever he will." This is not therapeutic expression. It is a kind of childish irresponsibility, and it too is nonsense. We have both a human and Christian obligation to respect the persons and personhood of other people; not, of course, to make a doormat of ourselves to the world, but to be caring and considerate human beings, and to curb our rotten pride and our still more rotten anger. We will sometimes fail, but this is quite different from making failing a virtue because we can't or don't want to control it as a vice.

# Confidence

## I

once heard the story of a supremely confident man who was out shooting one day; and when he had missed the bird which was the target, he was heard to murmur: "Isn't that remarkable? That bird continues to fly, even though he is shot through the heart!" Overconfidence in such a rather extreme case is not, however, the usual condition of the average person. And every once in a while the liturgy suggests that we should have confidence that the Christian life really can be lived in today's world, however remote it seems from the pressing realities which seem to be ever with us. I think that the greatest temptation in the Christian life today is not fear of persecution, or even of the grosser sins, but simply the remoteness of the spiritual, the feeling that today's world is too far removed from Christ and a Christian ethic for a genuine religious life to be possible in our twentieth century.

We are told, however, in the liturgy that despite our inevitable frailty, our worldliness, and infidelities, we should have confidence in our capacity to reflect Christ to our world. We believe that no thought of ours is ignored, no tear unheeded, no joy unnoticed. He is with us all days, in our joys and griefs, even to the consummation of the world. Of course we know such things, but we can't believe them in our heart of hearts. Yet what Newman called notional assent is not enough; our faith must *live* in our world. And our Lord continues to tell us what we must do: Share your bread with the hungry, shelter the oppressed and the homeless, clothe the naked, don't turn your back on your own, remove oppression and malicious speech from your lives, take care of the afflicted, and so on.

If we do these things, light will shine in the darkness, and God will be with us, and we *can* have a reasonable confidence amid the terrors of the world. The Gospel further tells us that we ourselves must be the light of the world, and that our light must shine before men.

We haven't been given an impossible job — a hard one, maybe, but not impossible. We must try to find lessons for living in the Gospels, and a frequent reading of them enables us to realize what it is all about. And we must be patient, not only with our neighbor but also with ourselves, because we are not going to become perfect overnight. As a matter of fact, we're not going to become perfect at all. But with the grace of God and some real human effort we can tidy up our world a bit, and we can tidy up our messy selves a lot.

One of my favorite authors, the previously cited G.K. Chesterton, has a saying: "Anything worth doing is worth doing badly." This, of course, is not a plea for shoddy performance but actually a conviction that it is better to do something rather than to do nothing at all. With the grace of God and some real human effort we can indeed be more loving and generous and sensitive in the circles in which we move. We can care for our needy brothers and sisters in our corner of the world.

Now, we're not going to remake the whole world, but we can improve the part of it in which we live and work and love and pray and suffer; and doing these things can give us the confidence that we are reacting as best we can to the mandates of our Blessed Lord.

Much has been made of the guilt and irresponsibility of human decision. Much has been made of human arrogance and how it has contributed to human downfall and misery. But many of our problems result from a failure to realize our worth, our dignity, our strength, our possibilities. Indeed, we do tend to sell ourselves short. We forget that we are children of divine love, that Christ can cure our blindness and our weakness. Our very existence is a testimony to that love. We have been purchased with a great price, and Christ reminds us that the very hairs of our head are numbered.

And the question might indeed be asked: Why are we not more joyously confident Christians? Of course we make mistakes, and sometimes they are spectacular. But the essential fact still remains that we are children of divine love, children of hope — and our lives should reflect this truth. Our infirmities should not claim our full attention if that kind of attentiveness is going to paralyze our efforts. The writer Jean Kerr once used a wonderful expression, referring to people who suffer "from delusions of adequacy." Sometimes, indeed, we may be falsely confident, but I think the greater risk is that we shall be unduly fearful.

We should be prudently aware of our limitations, but again the reality is not only what is but what can be. The character of Dulcinea in *Man of La Mancha* expresses this thought well when she asks poignantly, "Why do we associate reality with what is, rather than with what can be?" Potentiality and possibility in our lives may be rich, and we may need God's grace to do it, but we can bring many of the possibles in our lives to actuality. Our lives may be hobbled by addictive behavior to such things as food, nicotine, or alcohol. Our problem may be uncharity or insensitivity to others. It may be the highly fashionable rationalized selfishness of our time. But one thing is certain: The God who made water out of wine and apostles out of fishermen can make us more authentically human, and can rescue us from our lesser selves. The same God can bring to fruition the rich promise of which we are capable. We must bring to the art of living the same disciplined effort and confident hope that we bring to the less important enterprises of our technological world.

Let's keep in mind that our basic support system is an awareness of what we are and what we can be. Our faith should indeed engender a quiet confidence that we can meet the duties of life a day at a time; a quiet strength to remind us in turbulent moments that we shall not be overwhelmed; a quiet realization of the joy and beauty of life in our loves, and in the simple things of life. Ask for the confidence and the capacity to say "Can do" to the summons to the best that is in us.

Confidence is not whistling by the churchyard; it is realizing that our lives do not end there.

# Death

*O*NE winter, on my way back from Middleburg, Virginia, to Washington, D.C., I was driving through the mountains, when suddenly I came upon the sight of the frightful air crash of December 1, 1974, when a plane in a storm slammed into the Blue Ridge Mountains. It was as if a giant scythe had cut away the trees with almost clinical precision. And in an instant, ninety-two souls entered eternity.

It was brought home to me more forcefully when I saw from the road a little shoe in the snow. One moment ninety-two people had hopes and dreams. In another moment there was silence, and an empty shoe in the snow.

It made me realize how fragile is this thing called life, and how much we must foster that which is in us most imperishable. Death until recently, perhaps with the writing of Elisabeth Kübler-Ross, was the great unmentionable. It is to the secular mind the darkness at the end of the trail, the bludgeon of oblivion.

To a Christian, however, it should be the beginning and the homecoming. But how often we share the fears of those who have no hope, no faith, no expectation. We know our Redeemer lives, but our knowing does not add up to realization in the very depth of our being. Death, however, will come to us as it comes to all mankind, for it is not a brutal interruption but a logical consequence of life. It may not come in one awful moment at the top of a mountain in a snowstorm, but it will come.

And in that moment it will matter not how long the years but how great the years, how rich the moments. I remember a beautiful note written by the French writer Malsherbes to one M. DuPerier, when the latter lost a young daughter. It said, in part, that, rose that she was, she lived as roses live — that is, but "the space of a morning" *(l'espace d'un matin)*.

Our faith should prepare us for eternal life whether we live the space of a morning, or late into the evening of our years. It should remind us not to fear, because whether we live, or whether we die, we are the Lord's.

But of course we are not made of stone. We remember that Christ wept over Jerusalem, and at the tomb of Lazarus. It is not un-Christian to vent our grief when a loved one dies. It is natural and understandable to lament the fact that never in this life will we see again a beloved face or hear again a beloved voice. And we don't know why the Lord takes those with lives largely unlived, with dreams unrealized and hopes unfulfilled. We know only that our Father's undying love will be with us always, and that in his providential vision all will be well.

There is certainly mystery too in the death of the innocent by violence or accident. But the human spirit can suffer much, and still be enriched by grief. The poet Keats tells us how our sorrow itself can take on, in time, a kind of beauty. We know that what our loved ones have meant to us can never die; but the Christian is not limited to memory, as rich as those memories may be — for our Lord, who is the Resurrection and the life, reminds us in our loneliness and sorrow that he who believes in him will never die.

Death is indeed not something that happens to somebody else. We have no time, in the days that we have, for either the sinful, or even the second best. To think of death should be neither morbid nor depressing. It is the logical consequence of having lived.

The souls of the just are in the hands of God. They are gold tried in the furnace. And they shall indeed shine "and dart about like sparks through stubble." They are our loved ones. But they're the Lord's too.

# The Fallen-Away

*I*N one of the quietly sad moments of the New Testament, we read of a group of our Lord's friends who walked no more with him. They could not accept the reality of the Eucharist and became Christianity's first fallen-aways. Our Lord was sad at their departure, but he did not force their allegiance nor repudiate the Eucharist. He would not buy their love. And he asked the Apostles, "Will you also go away?"

Through the ages Christ's flock has suffered defection, and today is no exception. There are many who walk no more with him; many who have more or less left the Church; many who, in exaggerated independence, acknowledge no law or authority beyond their own appetites or wills. There are many who feel no obligation to attend Sunday Mass, and we would be less than candid were we to deny that church attendance has gone down, that standards have been let down.

I have heard young people say, "Well, I wouldn't even go to Sunday Mass if I didn't live at home." Now, I admit that liturgy should be made attractive and sermons interesting, and both often are not; but even if they're not, the Mass is not some form of entertainment. The intrinsic value of the Eucharist is what counts. Either this is the sacrifice which our Blessed Lord told us to enact until the end of time, or it is not.

The reason why the intrinsic value of the Eucharist

is more important than sensibility is that it is the sacrifice our Savior gave to the world. "Do this in memory of me," he told us. Anyone who judges value merely on a pleasure principle is in for trouble, and that is a fault of our time. Nothing in life is perpetual enchantment.

One of our popular expressions — "turned on" — is indicative of the subjectivism we tend today to bring to value judgments. How do I feel? How are my sensibilities and emotions stimulated? Well, what should we ask? Did Christ say this, or didn't he? Did he call this sin, or didn't he? Did he preach love and fidelity, or didn't he? Did he build a Church on the primacy of Peter, or didn't he? What is the objective value, no matter what I happen to feel? What is the value of the sacrifice of the Mass? Is it Christ's sacrifice, or is it not? And if it is, it is the sacrifice of Jesus Christ whether or not I ever existed, and its value is not diminished by my feelings, or my taste. Feelings and taste should be catered to in perhaps a choice of our amusements, in our choice of hobbies or television programs, but more than taste is involved in our spiritual welfare.

Of course there is stupidity, and even evil, within the Church. The Church is a Church of sinners, and because we are sinners, we need Christ's strength, and his love — and, yes, we need his prohibitions to curb our unruly selves.

And of course there is much goodness outside the Church, but can those who leave really do more for humanity or self outside? I am well aware that many, especially the young, have to resolve crises in faith, and I would agree that forced religion is no religion at all. But it is surprising that so many seem to assume for themselves an infallibility they deny the pope. But remember: In this era that has enshrined selfishness and feeling, the Church of Christ will endure to the end of time whether or not we are in it, and it will be there not only to give stability and love to those who stay, but it will be there for its children humble enough to find their way back. For the Church is life and love and strength, and it is the door to eternity.

I might add here too one postscript. Many of our young people today have drifted away for one or more reasons, among them parental neglect in failing to provide a Catholic education or a Catholic environment. If parents don't think religion is important in life, why should their children?

But sometimes, despite an excellent environment and a good Catholic education, young people leave anyway. However, a crisis in faith is not necessarily a permanent abandonment, and many defections are temporary in nature. Some young people have to travel a hard road to find the values by which they will eventually live. And many — with the help of your patience and your prayers — will find their way back to the richness of the faith.

# Reverence

*S*OME

years ago Harvey Cox wrote a very popular work called *The Secular City*, which supposedly caught the mood of the time and the religious spirit of contemporary man.

Contemporary religious feeling was thought to be free, spontaneous, unstructured, sincere, and highly individualistic. Cox pointed up the extremes. The older, in his view, tended to separate religious values from the marketplace; confine religion to the sanctuary; divorce morality from pressing social concerns such as war, poverty, and racism; emphasize the theoretical and the speculative, the otherworldly at the expense of The Secular City; and accept the institutional and structured elements of the faith as if a particular form or structure were as imperishable as the truth which animated it.

But I think perhaps the other extreme of a freewheeling faith is a greater danger in our time as the more recent writings of Harvey Cox suggest. The new secularistic faith is certainly not without its own dangers. It tends to emphasize the secular at the expense of the sacred. It is ill at ease with structure, permanence, doctrine, authority, or anything else that transcends human experience. It is often faith tailored to the human ego. It is highly, if selectively, personalistic. It is indeed very much involved in our world. It is, as the Spanish philosopher Ortega might call it, existential.

Secularistic faith tends not only to question but also to dismiss everything that is not seen as immediately relevant. It tends to dismiss hierarchy, formality, doctrine, and the familiar accouterments of traditional religion as anachronistic. It would see the cathedrals of Chartres and Rouen, not as monuments of faith and voluntary offerings of the human spirit, but as money badly spent. It dismisses churches themselves as barriers, titles as divisive, and the supernatural as illusory; and it often ends up with social concern not the main element of faith but the sole element of faith. It becomes, in short, a blessed sociology.

The new faith is a faith that accepts incarnation but rejects transcendence; it accepts a Christ whom it excessively humanizes but rejects the Trinity as intolerable mystery. Within the seminary, it is impatient with both philosophy and theology in favor of minimal moral maxims that will enable one to hurry to the barricades to right all wrongs. It is more pontifical than the Supreme Pontiff it often questions, more self-righteous than the clericalism it laments; but it supposedly is "with it."

I should like to suggest that we do not have to choose between an aloof faith that has no regard for worldly concerns, and a worldly faith that eventually dispenses with God and the supernatural. I should like to suggest also that anything associative or collective will assume structural or institutional form but that the form must be reasonably responsive to the spirit that creates it. This attitude accepts change but does not deify it.

I should like to suggest further that ignorant enthusiasm helps very little; that study, theory, or its prayerful equivalent or contemplation must be preparatory to fruitful action. A sense of reverence for the sacred is quite compatible with social concern. I should like to suggest also that the search for the transcendent and the eternal is part of the human experience; that mystery is not a dirty word. There is mystery in birth, and love, and death. I would like to suggest too that reality is not limited to that which we have reduced to textbook dimensions — that which we have weighed and seen and counted — but extends also to the great realm of the intangibles.

I think that the new secularism is not too wide — rather, it is too narrow — in defining the human if it excludes the contemplative, the transcendent, and the mysterious. I don't think a priest has to run around in tennis shoes, jeans, and a turtleneck sweater and have ten-year-olds call him by his first name in order to be relevant. On the other hand, I don't think that the rectory has to be an inaccessible Olympus guarded by a formidable housekeeper either.

I don't think we are obliged to be immediately suspect of any authoritative suggestion or decision, but we certainly don't have to believe that adopted political forms of the Roman Empire are sacred and unchanging. We don't have to accept the Eucharist as a shared meal, and ridicule it as the presence of our Lord.

Of course we must be concerned about our world. It is the only one we have, but we must worship the most high God and live and preach his Gospel. We must be reverent and prayerful men and women if we would be effective and keep that sense of the sacred in our minds. Rudolf Otto, reflecting this Old Testament verticality, referred to God as the Wholly Other, the Infinite, the Transcendent.

But the dilemma is a false one. Our God is incarnate, Emmanuel; but he is also Yahweh, our God who is, and was, and shall be.

# Suffering

## *T*HOSE

of us who deal with people on a pastoral level are painfully aware of how many people out there are hurting. Our mental hospitals, homes for battered spouses, shelters for abused children or runaways; our bruised derelicts huddling over grates to keep warm, or clutching their cardboard shelters around them; our accidents, illnesses, and anxieties that bedevil even the affluent — all these at times are sober reminders of the inevitability of suffering that is part and parcel of the human condition. And when we look outside of our comparatively safe and secure environments, we see just how much illness, warfare, strife, disease, and poverty cast dark shadows over the lives of people.

We can react to all of this by simply tuning it out, selfishly living in a world in which such depressing realities have neither claim nor recognition. There's a wonderful story told about a Maryknoll sister who was visited by her college classmate. She was working in the Far East with the cancerous poor, under extremely depressing conditions. They both had come from rather affluent homes and the visitor said to her classmate: "I wouldn't do that for a million dollars." The nun replied: "Neither would I."

We can believe with the cynic, of course, that life is a shipwreck, and that — hopeless though we may be — we survive that shipwreck as best we can until the bludgeon of oblivion, death, cancels our pain. Or we can play the games that anesthetize us to our own world and its misery. But when the games people play are over, there must be something real within, a life of the spirit, an inner strength, a sharing in an understanding of the suffering of Christ.

I mentioned games. People playing games may be in pursuit of wealth, power, or beauty; or, perhaps, distraction, oblivion, drugs, or recreational sex — such dreariness. In F. Scott Fitzgerald's *The Great Gatsby* there's a wonderful description of the pleasure-loving Tom and Daisy: "They broke up things and people, and then retreated into their vast carelessness, or whatever else it was that kept them together, and let other people clean up the mess they had made."

Materialists don't merely misunderstand spiritual things; they misunderstand material things. They mistake the temporary for the ultimate, the pleasurable for the satisfying. Happiness is not glandular; it's not packaged as a commodity. Faith can still breathe life into our dry bones, for whether we live or die we're still the Lord's. Faith is not a commitment; it's the quiet strength to endure. It is that taking up of our cross daily and uncomplainingly.

Speaking of "uncomplainingly" reminds me of Mark Twain's observation that when some people discharge an obligation you can hear it all over the world. Faith is not always raising widow's sons to life or giving sight to the blind. It is often the greater but quieter triumph of grace in the troubled heart. The life of the spirit does not numb us to life, but it can bring a quiet and serene joy of soul to cope with the inevitabilities of life.

Senator Charles Percy once asked Mother Teresa: "Don't you feel discouragement at trying to combat the poverty and the suffering in the world?" And she answered quite simply: "God has not called me to be successful but to be faithful." She lives in the world's misery, but she is serene in God's love.

Now, maybe the light of the spirit offers no quick victories as we experience life a day at a time. Perhaps we just undramatically bear one another's burdens, make no great decisions in the councils of the great, and perhaps not even a big dent in the misery of the world. But if the Christian life, like politics, is the art of the possible, then this Christian life — even in our time, and even if flawed — is still happily possible.

The great French writer François Mauriac, commenting upon the inevitable anguish of life, once wrote: "Today in the evening of my life I know the final answer. It is Jesus Christ who alone quiets the radical anguish that is in us, an anguish so much a part of the human condition that is with us from the cradle to the grave: the torment of loneliness, the vacillating shadows of those we love as they leave us in the horrible mysteries of death; the limitless gratifications of our ego of being one who loves but is not loved; or who is loved but does not love; the trials of old age and the decline of strength and the decline of the mind and the approach of ineluctable dissolution. If these do not constitute a radical anguish in the human heart, there is still the anguish of being in the world, and not knowing where to find peace and happiness."

It is indeed Christ who is meant to satisfy this deep anguish that is part of life. Some, of course, have been bruised more than others. We are all wounded birds, but most of us can still fly. Some of us, as the poet Yeats says, carry our precipices with us. Some of us complicate our situations by self-pity, and others by pretending the real does not exist. But it is infantile to think that pain is not a dimension of human life. Both faith and reason remind us, however, that pain is not a negation of human life.

One of the most vulnerable aspects, I think, of our secular culture is its inability to deal with pain, suffering, and frustration. The antidote seems to be a search for forgetfulness and oblivion. Karl Marx once said that religion was the opium of the people. Some tend to reverse it, and make opium the religion of the people. But you can't tune the world out — not for long. It is relentlessly present. Perhaps we just come to realize (by increasing the grace and strength of the sacramental life) the role of the cross in our lives in making us more compassionate, sensitive, and caring human beings.

Perhaps too there is something in suffering that is analogous to the phenomenon of pruning in horticulture. There's something surgical in the excision of our selfishness. Perhaps we see God as a divine sculptor, hammering our protesting reality into the desired shape. Perhaps we do try to understand anguish and reach out a hand in the darkness. Life, of course, is not all great moments — and not all of the victories, as often has been observed, are great victories. But to know the wisdom of the cross is to know its triumph. It's not masochism. We don't seek misery for its own sake. We simply try to incorporate inevitable suffering into the life that we have, and try to keep realizing that Calvary leads to personal resurrection. And that resurrection, no matter how dimly we perceive it, is still our joyful destiny.

The cross is our triumph, not a symbol of futility, and perhaps we, in spending our hour in Gethsemane, acquire a kind of wisdom we find nowhere else.

# Anxiety

*I*<sub>T</sub> is one of the thundering clichés of our time to refer to our age as the age of anxiety and frustration. I would like to mention Drucker's words — "The erosion of continuities" — to refer to the loss of stability, a stability that was formerly afforded by church, home, and nation. They seem to be less capable of eliciting that creative and faithful response they once did. Yeats captures this anxiety when he says: "Things fall apart, the centre cannot hold; / Mere anarchy is loosed upon the world. . . . / The best lack all conviction, while the worst / are full of passionate intensity."

Women, for instance, feel obliged to apologize for being only housewives. Men feel ineffectual if they have not scrambled to the top of the anthill by age forty. Both often have the rather disturbing malaise that somehow life is passing them by. And more interesting is the story of those who *are* at the top of the heap by the age of forty.

One of the tribal rites of spring is the Academy Awards ceremony in which the movie industry indulges in its relentless and indefatigable narcissism. Each of five authors of a forgettable documentary must thank everyone who has influenced his or her life since the age of seven; and top actors and actresses, unaccustomed to such bit parts as saying "thank you" feel obliged to advise us on the state of the nation, the insensitivity of Kansas farmers, or the fate of the sperm whale.

But most of all, the successes seem to be more anxiety-ridden than the failures. Many seem to spend several days a week in analysis, and complain of the religion of their early years (which, of course, they have discarded). Bruised and repressed, their sensitive egos manage only to survive through their analysts. They have sought relief on the couch, psychiatric and otherwise, and, still being unable to cope, are often unhappy — desperately!

One comic genius who swept the awards almost hid in a closet, as terrified by his honors as much as the proud person is terrified by his failure. But what is interesting is how a frustrated world reacts to frustrated heroes. Our generation does not have ticker-tape parades for people who fly oceans. The new hero is the klutz, someone who can't walk across the room without knocking over a coffee table, and we tend to identify with this hero of ineptitude.

The young women on the campus now have the Annie Hall look with the electric-socket hairdos and fashions that look as if they walked into wet sheets on their mother's clothesline.

Perhaps I'm reading too much into all of this, but it

is appalling how restless and unhappy a supposedly liberated and affluent people are. The poor and the hungry and the oppressed and the sick and the persecuted present no mystery at all. They have lots to be unhappy about.

But when I say we have to rediscover faith and moral values like those of the early Christians, I mean that we must set the Lord ever before our sight to feel this quiet strength. I think we should know his words, rather than base our lives on vague perceptions or unwarranted assumptions. That's why I have repeatedly counseled that a chapter a day of the New Testament is an easy means of finding out what Christ really said.

We don't have to be members of the Fad of the Month Club — just more faithful Christians who pattern our lives on the values outlined by Christ. The spurious faiths of our world not only do not provide an answer to sorrow, they don't even teach us how to live with joy. If we read the Acts of the Apostles, we discover a precious time in the lives of this small caring, worshiping community. They have little of this world's goods. They are despised both by the orthodox religious establishment and by imperial Rome, but they are at peace in the depths of their souls.

The same Lord has the same strength to make us at peace in the turmoil of our world. We must bring our errant selves back from the frantic acquisitive world of contemporary success to spiritual and moral stability. If we shut out some of the noise of the world, perhaps we can hear the words, "Let not your hearts be troubled."

# Caesar's Things

## $O_{NE}$

of the more difficult things in our world is trying to solve the question of contradictory political and religious allegiances. To what degree is the Christian at home in the world? To what degree do we really know the answer in saying blithely, "Render to Caesar the things that are Caesar's and to God the things that are God's"?

Certainly I think this uncertainty is markedly accentuated in the contemporary South American experience, in which we have the so-called Marxist theologians espousing revolution as a kind of Christ-derived attitude that would destroy a world of privilege by violence before a world of justice can be built in peace.

It's not always easy to make the separation of our two worlds, and we're increasingly concerned with the subject of moral propriety in government. It has often been said that the people get the kind of government they deserve, and therefore if a society exhibits moral sloppiness in particular, that same tone will be reflected in society at large, and in its chosen representatives.

The European response has often been to have a Christian political party — a party supposedly animated by Christian principles and represented by practicing Christians. Most of us Americans, I feel, are uneasy with such a solution, and I think justifiably so. In many cases, those political parties seemed to be based, perhaps disproportionately, on a fear of Communism, and any effort to induce any kind of social concern or social betterment is sometimes equated with Communism.

I think most of us prefer to evaluate professional expertise and basic integrity, and choose our representatives on the basis of a political outlook that is more concerned with competence rather than piety. We feel uncomfortable with too close an identification with the political and the religious.

The amount of initiative reserved to the private sector, or the range of social services we think government should provide, is indeed much more reflective perhaps of our economic than our religious status, and, of course, that's our privilege. But morality and integrity are still involved. We shouldn't be willing to buy the liberal but cynical philosophy that anything a person does after hours is acceptable. Integrity of character cannot be conveniently broken up, and it is insolence for a dissolute man to expect to be chosen to make value judgments, if his moral value judgments show flagrant deficiency.

This demand for integrity, of course, can be carried too far; but, in general, aspiration to public service does invite, and should invite, public scrutiny. Character, however, is not enough. I think we do have an ethical obligation to vote, to participate in the government of our land; but we're not obliged to choose an inept saint anymore than we are obliged to choose a clever lecher. Professional expertise is indispensable, and personal sanctity is no substitute for it.

Moral imperatives too cannot always be reproduced in the political order, for many fallible judgments are involved. But voting is more of an obligation than a privilege, because it recognizes a sense of responsibility that extends far beyond post-election grumbling. It *is* our responsibility to exercise the influence we can — if we can, when we can — toward good and responsible government.

The French have a saying that the absent are always wrong. I think our responsibility increases with the relative importance of our voice. Some say: "Well, politics is a dirty business and I'll have nothing to do with it!" That is what the world calls a cop-out. If politics is a dirty business, it is because the negligent and the indifferent have let the unprincipled take over. Political responsibility is indeed not only our privilege; it is an ethical dimension of our citizenship.

The reason I have not equated this, of course, with a specific party affiliation is quite obvious. No party has a monopoly on political probity. The Catholic-country concept is hardly more helpful. History has not recorded that states have really profited by being officially Catholic or Protestant, for religion in such countries becomes often a cultural accouterment rather than a spiritual commitment.

What does seem necessary is to recognize that we are political animals, as Aristotle says, and if we are, we do have the obligation by mature evaluation and decision to create the finest political climate in which religious values (as well as other social and cultural values) may thrive.

Intregrity is important and essential, but there is no holy nation and there is no holy party. We must decide, and in doing so to the best of our ability, we will be rendering to Caesar the things that are Caesar's and to God the things that are God's. And maybe *not* being certain we have made the right choice is better than being certain that we have.

# Responsibility

$V_{ERY}$ frequently in the New Testament our Lord tells us to lead watchful, responsible, principled lives. And he doesn't seem to be talking to the committed sinner as much as to the lukewarm and the lax, the casual sinner who will put everything in order — but not till tomorrow; who will reform his life, do what he knows to be done . . . tomorrow.

A farsighted steward knows that for him and for everybody else there may be no tomorrow — that the Lord may come unexpectedly. He tells us to expect the unexpected by being what we ought to be *today*, by doing what we ought to do *today*, by starting what we ought to start *today*, by finishing what we ought to finish *today*, and by leaving behind what ought to be left behind *today*.

Our Lord is telling us, in essence, that moral irresponsibility consists not in outright repudiation but often merely in slovenly or deferred performance. And our Lord — in submitting himself to baptism, for instance — illustrates dramatically how he shares the human condition, despite his divinity. He is innocence itself, and yet he consents to be baptized. The Father proclaims his divinity; the Holy Spirit hovers in the form of a dove. When the Christian is baptized, he has not submitted to an empty ritual, an introduction into civil society; rather, he is literally incorporated into the family of God.

And if baptism is only the first step in the educative process of the Christian, then we are expected to grow in Christ. We are expected to grow in awareness and in responsible, principled behavior. And that is not an easy job in today's world. It is not an easy job because in the interest of a supposed enlightenment, we have become nonjudgmental. We're not supposed to say anything is wrong anymore. Being nonjudgmental seems to be the ultimate compliment. We go all the way from genes to environment to rationalized delinquency, as if that which explains automatically excuses. And often the explanation is as faulty and as fatuous as the excusing is eloquent.

Not too long ago a lengthy discussion took place in the public press about teenage pregnancy, and one would actually get the impression that one gets pregnant as one catches a cold. Nowhere was it suggested that sexual promiscuity is simply immoral and irresponsible behavior, and that such irresponsible behavior is to be discouraged by moral training. Nowhere was it suggested that information alone is not moral conviction. The implication was quite simply that the environment was a determinant rather than an influence. And God forbid that we say an abandonment of one's responsibilities is wrong or evil.

Now, I have nothing against the study of psychological motivation or the study of environmental deprivation as a background for delinquency; but what is obscured in this modern approach is the elementary ethical truth that we should not commit any act — sexual or otherwise — for which we are not prepared to accept responsibility; and that as responsible human beings there are some things to which we should simply not adjust. There is a rational and demonstrable difference between cruelty, brutality, murder, cheating, fraud, and rape, and the opposite values of love, friendship, sympathy, fidelity, generosity, and compassion.

The *ought* in life can be derived from the *is*. We simply have to recognize that not just any kind of conduct is similarly beneficial to the human condition; that values are not entirely subjective, however great the subjective element may be. Our tastes in food are subjective, but there is nothing subjective about nutrition. To be incorporated into the family of God is indeed to *be* judgmental. It's to be decisive, not prematurely or ignorantly decisive, but decisive and judgmental. And it is to act in those convictions that are logically arrived at, or arrived at as a result of our acceptance of divine revelation.

The Ten Commandments certainly are judgmental. God doesn't say observe them if they're convenient, or observe them if they're not otherwise bruising to your psyche or to your sense of fulfillment. The opponent says, "What about Christ's admonition: 'Judge not lest ye be judged'?" Of course we should have sympathy for the sinner; but today we are asked to have sympathy for the sin, and we've become insensitive to a sense of responsibility in the family, in the office, in the department store, in the marketplace, and in government; and irresponsibility is not even intelligent selfishness.

I see the baptism exemplified by our Savior as incorporating us into a distinctive Christian value system — and that means, not that we all are saints, but that we should try to be. Notice, however, that our Lord tells us in effect: "Fear not, little flock, I have for you a kingdom when I come, however unexpectedly, and I come not to destroy but to fulfill and not to kill but to introduce everlasting life."

# Joy

*T*HERE'S
a theme in the New Testament that seems often to be neglected, and that is the theme of joy. The concordance to the Bible lists twenty-six occasions when our Blessed Lord spoke directly of joy. And I think because we forget that the Christian life is, or should be, a joyous life, we should reflect on it more than we do.

Christianity's greatest secret is that we are children not of death but of the Resurrection. Puritans and Jansenists over the years have done much to make the religious faith seem more like an oppressive burden. It was once said that Puritans objected to the Elizabethan sport of bear-baiting, not because it caused pain to the bear, but because it brought pleasure to the spectators.

And pleasure itself, in this dour counterfeit of Christianity, was thought to be evil.

Saint Paul, for instance, despite shipwreck and imprisonment, ill health and harassment, is a happy man in the Lord's service. He tells the Romans to calm down; that if we live, we live for the Lord; if we die, we die for the Lord — and therefore whether we live or die, we belong to the Lord. In his Second Epistle to the Corinthians Paul says, "In all of our many troubles, my cup is full of consolation and overflows with joy." In Galatians he says, "The truth of the spirit is joy." He tells the Philippians that they are to be partakers of his joy, and the Colossians to face whatever the future brings, not only with courage and patience, but with joy. In short, he seems to realize he serves a Lord who promises joy and reward a hundredfold to him and all those who follow the Lord generously, faithfully, and lovingly.

One of the great glories of the personal visits of the Holy Father is the example he gives to the whole world (to the secular world as well as to the religious world): the picture of a happy man — happy in his humanness, happy in his priesthood, confident in his faith. And God knows, he was not insulated from the harshness of life, surviving Nazis and Communists in one lifetime. That could possibly make a dour — or sour — bitter man, but not if he has the joyous faith of a John Paul. In many cases he seems again to have actually been enriched by trials, matured by them, and to have developed a great sense of compassion and understanding with which he brings this great pastoral sensitivity to the flock.

We must recognize ourselves as the architects of our joyous life, aided by the grace of God. We need neither a superfluity of things nor the bizarre cults that would nourish the spirit by appealing to eccentricity. We must feel the quiet strength and joy of a divine presence. We need be but more faithful Christians who pattern their lives on the values of Jesus Christ.

If we read the Acts of the Apostles we read of a precious time in the lives of this early, caring, worshiping community after our Lord's Resurrection. They have very little of the world's goods; they are despised both by the orthodox religious establishment and by imperial Rome. But there is a wholeness, a joy in the depths of their souls. And the same Lord has the same strength to make us more at peace amid the turmoil of our world. The Holy Spirit can breathe new life into the dry bones of our casual faith, and can endow us with the same quiet joy and strength. And of course we should be joyous people, not because we're oblivious to the trials of the world, not because we're insensitive to reality, but because Christianity does not end on Calvary.

Why is it that the Christian life is so little identified with joy? That's what it's all about: the love of God and the love of man that look forward to the time when death itself shall be no more, when God will wipe all tears from our eyes. God asks us to love him, and to trust him, and — most of all — to realize that he loves us. Saints realize that.

I remember hearing a story once of a little girl who was asked who the saints were; and thinking of the stained-glass windows in the parish church she said, "The saints are those who let the light shine through" — which of course is not a bad definition. "Out of the mouths of babes thou hast perfected praise." Perhaps we have no blueprint of eternity; but we do know the imperishable qualities of love, friendship, generosity, and courage — and all of those other things that make lives worthwhile.

So as Resurrection children let us sing no sad songs, and let us not lament the fall of civilization as we know it in the western world. Even a Nietzsche could say that the one who survives the twentieth century will need a lot of eternity in his soul. We are called to be that kind of person.

My late acquaintance Arnold Toynbee, the British historian, noted that almost every civilization he studied died from within, from a death of the spirit rather than from external assault. Now, if we're not spiritual men and women, courageous enough to live with quiet firmness the truths we profess to believe, then I think we deserve the joyless life of those who have no hope and have built their towers of Babel on the things of the world which they have loved and served. But the followers of Christ should be a happy people.

It's true that many people view the Church and Christian life in terms of rigor, repression, and joylessness. But discipline is not repression, any more than indulgence is happiness. It is imperative in these days of stress and change that we remember that our Christian heritage is a heritage of joy, and that the Christian life can be lived in a hostile world.

I remember seeing — shortly after the election of the Holy Father — a picture of John Paul and Archbishop Runcie walking side by side down the long aisle of Becket's Canterbury Cathedral. They knelt together, and in a historic moment prayed together for their people and their world. We of the flocks of the faithful should do the same, that Christ's life might be lived more fully in our world. John Paul gives to us, of the larger family of God, an example of the unity that should characterize the world of faith. We, the people, must bring God's love and God's joy into a world too long sad, too long embattled, too long estranged. With his help and with his grace, that new work may begin with us.

# Loneliness

S*OME* time ago I heard a ballad that had this line: "I can't stand the sound of silence." I think loneliness is another one of those great concerns of our time. The very young search for the hand of the father, or the warm embrace of the mother; the adolescent moves into his new world, beset with many insecurities. It's the age when parental love can often be an anchor when it tries to be a sail. Adults fortunate enough to love and be loved see themselves threatened constantly in a world in which the coronary or the auto accident can destroy that warmth and security in one terrible moment.

There is the loneliness of the widow, the divorced, the deserted, and the disappointed. And in life's twilight, the aged often feel a subdued terror akin to night fears of childhood. Insecurity and loneliness seem to be so much a part of the human condition. It was part of our Lord's passion that he should feel such agony in Gethsemane. And Gethsemane will be a part of our lives too. But I should like to suggest — while conceding loneliness at one time or another to be universal — that to be alone is not necessarily to be lonely. Solitude and silence are values in our culture that seem to have been lost. There are creative insights and a kind of awareness that come only in solitude. There are depths of understanding and compassion that we come to feel only after suffering alone, and we can grow and be creative in our loneliness.

A man, for instance, who sees his beloved companion of life's years buried, feels that he can never live those lonely years in which places and things constantly evoke memories of the beloved. The parent who sees a child cut down in the springtime of life, even amid the support and love of other members of the family, can find no words to express the anguish that a dear young face will never be seen again. Then there is the lesser loneliness that comes from the uniqueness of our own personalities, the love lost, or the love that never was.

We have to be complete human beings before we can be anything else to anyone else. We have to be complete, authentic human beings of character and sensitivity, not designed by nature and grace to spend our lives leaning on somebody else, no matter how dear, no matter how close. We have to be men and women of faith with a devoted sense of love of God and man, and the realization that Christ will help us to live our uniqueness.

The sharpness of our perceptions must be honed by

a sacramental life and a life of prayer that will be constantly enriched, that will give us conviction about life and death, love and friendship, honor and fidelity, joy and sorrow, change and disappointment. We must never stop growing — and if it be God's will that we do things alone, our lives can still be meaningful and joyous.

I remember in my youth (because I do have an extraordinary memory!) hearing a neighbor commenting on a slightly less than happy marriage, saying, "She just wanted to have 'Mrs.' on her tombstone." This, of course, was before the unpronounceable Ms. was designed to give a comfortable anonymity and calculated confusion to the whole business.

Now, it may well be that the lady in question would have done much better to live alone. And I can assure you that living alone is not as unpleasant as popular myths would have it.

Silence and solitude are not loved in our noisy world, but they are not necessarily evil. Gibran once said, "Let there be spaces in your togetherness." I think we should realize that there is a dimension of our existence in which we will always be alone — and then try by logic and grace to develop ourselves as persons. Next, I think we should try to help those who are genuinely lonely — to reach out in the darkness.

Look how the old and the sick are neglected in our society. We have to get rid of our aged lest we be inconvenienced. We visit them rarely, and assuage our guilt with holiday candy and flowers. We are so callously indifferent to the loneliness of their sunset years. And how lonely are many of the sick in our society. The world's noise should not have to hide us from ourselves. Inevitably even our dearest ones will go, and if it be God's will that someday we face life alone, we will be less lonely if we think of the needs of others instead of inundating ourselves in self-pity.

Let us ask God to enrich us in self, but without making us selfish, and to be more aware of others without losing sight of the precious dignity we possess individually as children of God. And let us be ever mindful of him who will be the ultimate cure for all loneliness.

# Mood of the Time

*I*

once heard an expression, "He who marries the spirit of the times will soon be a widower." As mentioned elsewhere in this book, I think one of the obvious truths is that there are fashions in thought, as there are fashions in clothes. Every age has its style, its mental and physical furniture. Like the air we breathe, we absorb its beliefs and values, and unless we have a value system — a stable and fixed set of convictions, presumably arrived at after sufficient thought and analysis — the chances are that we will be strongly influenced.

I think people today are particularly concerned about the young whose experience and training have not yet equipped them to be capable of understanding the pressures of their time. We see them as swayed, and they are shaken. They are indecisive like the man described in the axiom: "He sets his watch after every clock he passes."

I think the greatest fear a young person seems to have is appearing to be different. How much experimentation with drugs, for instance, has been occasioned, not by profound disillusion with their world, but by a curiosity bred by one's environment — an environment in which peer pressure is so important.

Witness, for instance, in this age (which emphasizes freedom and individuality) such meticulous casualness in dress, as well as uniformity. The jeans shouldn't be too new, the shoes too clean, the hair too short; to summarize, the generation which abhors uniforms and regimentation slavishly adopts the uniforms of unconformity with an inflexible rigor. In this age of casualness, one wonders how many hours must be spent in front of a mirror before the meticulous casualness is achieved.

Those of you who have seen films like *American Graffiti* and *Summer of '42* probably feel a certain nostalgia for other times and other structures, patterns, lifestyles. I remember reading about survivors of the *Titanic* fighting in a lifeboat because a male survivor was smoking a cigarette in the presence of ladies. Can you imagine anyone being preoccupied by such a triviality in the midst of a disaster that took more than fifteen hundred lives? Our sensibilities are not easily exacerbated these days by costume or behavior. The basic question is, "How much should the Christian adapt himself to his times?" How much should he be "with it," as the saying goes? How great is the obligation to be *au courant* of the latest moods, and the latest fads, and the latest customs? How much should we consider adjustment, which John Dewey spoke of so often, as being so desirable?

I think perhaps the Christian should be animated more often by a divine discontent, rather than by a desire to adjust. We are always, as the theologian Karl Rahner said, in a diaspora situation — on the outside looking in, never completely absorbed by the secular world and its concerns. Of course the obvious observation would be that we can't turn back the clock. We can't escape into a safer world of the past. There aren't those safe harbors that we thought existed. Nor can we escape into an imaginary world of the future. This is our place and our time. It may not be the best of times, the best of places; but it's ours, and here it is that we must work out our salvation — and we've got to do the best we can.

I often think of one phrase of our Lord. It's one of the bitterest things I think he ever uttered in the New Testament; and it was actually directed not to the evil but to the lukewarm: "I would that thou were either hot or cold; but because thou art neither hot nor cold, I will begin to vomit thee out of my mouth." Our Blessed Lord wants us to be men and women of principle and conviction. We should adjust to reality in the sense that we have to consider the real world and its problems, however distasteful at times that confrontation may be, and we have to recognize that what shocked us twenty years ago may perhaps not shock an open society nowadays.

But we shouldn't worry too much about the peripheral things; and we shouldn't absolutize the peripheral anymore than we should jettison the essential

102

The Christian does not have to adjust, nor should he adjust, to the squalid ethical values of an essentially pagan society. It has been said that a Christian civilization simply does not exist, that we must create a Christian civilization. Faith, of course, is not a popularity contest, and the best Christian is not the one who has accommodated himself comfortably to what is fashionable but the one who preserves a divine discontent with his world — and who still accepts the validity of the distinction between good and evil.

I think the casual Christian is an infelicitous term with which to identify the supposed noncommitted or non-Church Christian. I think the uncommitted Christian is often a progressively discernible secularist who dislikes the Ten Commandments because it is fashionable to bribe and to steal; to fornicate and to commit adultery; to destroy innocent life, whether it be unborn or aged; to look out for the self no matter how many other people are starving or hurting; to falsify, to misrepresent, and to mistake, above all, prevalence for justification — as if popularity were equivalent to moral acceptability.

A New Testament Christianity posits standards, whether we like them or not. A New Testament morality was not popular in our Lord's time, and it probably won't be popular in ours. Our problem today is not that our world is not Christian but that Christians aren't Christians. It might be said too that our problem is behavioral, because it is antecedently intellectual. We don't know what our Lord said, because the New Testament is not read, nor studied, nor loved as the Word of God.

103

We tend also to rationalize almost any kind of behavior on the grounds that a merciful God will understand. Well, there's no doubt about divine comprehension. It's not a question of divine comprehension but of human behavior, and the fact that some kind of behavior directly contravenes divine command. God indeed understands, but the God of mercy is also a God of justice — a God of standards, if you will, whose demands for honesty and integrity and fidelity are not mysteries. Let us ask our God for the vision to see his Word in our lives and in our world, and for the strength to live those conditions without rewriting that Word to suit ourselves.

Let us see, for instance, that fidelity to a cause, a faith, a vocation, a marriage partner, a task, is more important than how we feel. Let us differentiate fulfillment from rationalized selfishness, and a concerned faith in the most high God from blessed sociology or a mindless activism. Let us build a renewed faith around God's Word, in the Eucharist, both as meal and presence, and around a solicitude for the family of man, spelled out not in rhetoric but in service. We may not move mountains, but maybe — just maybe — we can nudge the earth a bit.

The French have a saying, "My glass is not large, but I drink from my glass." I use what talents I have; and I think that's what we should do. I've often said that the Christian life, like politics, is the art of the possible. We do what we can, with what we have, when we can, and as well as we can.

# Humility

*T*HE
greatest or perhaps the most influential sermon in the history of the world was the Sermon on the Mount, when the beatitudes were given to the world. The first of these beatitudes, humility, is something we might well ponder. *Beatitudo* in Latin means not only blessedness but happiness — and it's rather significant that in giving us a formula for sanctity, our Blessed Lord was giving us a formula for happiness also.

The first suggestion is directed against selfishness and arrogance, against prideful assertion of self to the detriment of others. We have books written today on how to be number one, how to intimidate others; they're based on a theory of human nature, popularized by the philosopher Hobbes, that we are combative, predatory creatures, destined not only for competition but also for strife. We are beasts of prey — wolves fighting one another. And here comes from the ancient world the Carpenter of Nazareth — apparently not overwhelmed by the power of imperial Rome, nor by the "flatulent newspeak" of our time — telling us that human beings should be brothers and sisters and friends and servants to one another. I'm not suggesting, of course, that Hobbes antedated our Blessed Lord. I'm suggesting merely that two enduring philosophies of life are in rather sharp contrast. Humility, I believe, is a most misunderstood virtue, because it's not abject self-deprecation.

It doesn't consist in a beautiful woman calling herself ugly, or in an intelligent man calling himself stupid; for humility is a virtue, and a virtue must be built on truth or it's no virtue at all.

Humility is simply the basic recognition of oneself as a child of God. Mary of the *Magnificat*, for instance, can say quite simply, "Henceforth all generations shall call me blessed." And Christ who proclaimed, "Learn of me for I am meek and humble of heart," did not hesitate to say also, "I am the way, the truth, and the life."

For Christ, the Son of God, to say he was less than the Son of God would not be humility — it would have been falsehood. When someone mentions humility we somehow conjure up the image of a Uriah Heap, the fawning sycophant with folded hands and downcast eyes who invites the world to walk all over him (although he doesn't really think that they should, and would be quite angry if they did).

Humility is really the virtue of the strong, not the weak. The humble man knows his place and takes it. He plays neither God nor the fool. The humble Christ drove the money changers out of the temple and castigated the hypocrites. The humble man — if he is supposed to rule — rules; and when he is supposed to serve, he serves; but even in his most triumphant moments, the humble man remembers that all he is, and all that he has, is from God. He does not mistake the gifts of God for an attainment of self.

Actually, the humble person doesn't consider himself a noun and the rest of the world adjectives. He works out his salvation knowing that in God's sight his brother and sister are just as good as he is. He respects others; he doesn't use them for his own purpose; he is not unduly sensitive to slights — seeing in the most innocent observations subtle attacks on his prideful self.

Pride is not only the most obvious of vices; it's also the most insidious. It insinuates itself into home, office, cloister, or marketplace with effortless ease. The humble man is considerate of others, whereas the proud recognizes others as having duties, himself as having rights. He is the neglectful, the inconsiderate, the unpunctual, the unforgiving, and the forgetful, because the vision of self blinds him to the sight of others.

Like Christ washing the feet of the Twelve Apostles, we should welcome opportunities to serve, to humble the imperious self, because a humble person is really a happy person, for he sees both the joys and the sorrows of life in perspective, and his role is almost in focus. Poverty of spirit is not mere poverty or deprivation; it's learning from Christ a little more about successful living and our place in God's world — a kind of spiritual geography, if you will. It reveals to us where home is — and how far or close we are to home.

# Sin

*I*N the twentieth century one of the most unpopular subjects to the modern pagan mind is the subject of sin. The modern pagan hasn't ceased to sin, but he has ceased to call it sin. He's changed his labels but not his morals. People have sinned in every age, but we try to explain it away by a kind of verbal gymnastics. We blame our environment, our educational system, or perhaps vitamin deficiency; and many of the old sins are now being explained away as new diseases. Shakespeare's character Edmund in *King Lear* says: "This is the excellent foppery of the world, that when we are sick in fortune, often the surfeit of our own behavior, we make guilty of our disasters the sun, the moon, and the stars: as if we were villains [by] necessity, fools by heavenly compulsion; knaves, thieves, and treachers by spherical predominance; drunkards, liars, and adulterers by an enforced obedience of planetary influence. . . ."

It's quite true, of course, that in advanced stages, alcoholism, for instance, is a disease in which the force of will may be minimized. But we can't keep escaping into pathology to explain delinquency. In the ages of faith, men sinned; but they knew they were sinning, and didn't try to explain away their guilt. Today, it's a little indecent even to mention sin. People are said to be merely responding to their environment, expressing themselves, or finding themselves.

Thomas Merton once said that every event in a person's life plants something in his soul; just as the wind carries thousands of invisible winged pollen, so time brings encounter and opportunity. And how we react to people and events is crucially important. God's grace accompanies us along the way; but we must respond — and, in a sense, sin is a lack of response to God's grace.

It's fashionable, of course, today to duck responsibility, to blame pathology, bad parenting perhaps, or our stars (as Edmund suggests above) for the messes we often make of our lives. But if we are the willing victim of our sin, our selfishness, our undisciplined appetites; if freedom is wild destructiveness or quiet folly — then the seeds of grace can die in our cold and unloving souls.

In reflective and prayerful silence from time to time, we should look into the depths of our hearts, and we may see sin there — selfishness, malice, or unchecked carelessness — spiritual laziness. And instead of whining about our bad luck, we should look into the depths of our souls, and see what we can change, and what we ought to change. It's really false modesty to think that we are not capable of greater things. It's a false humility to think that a loving Christ would not have the time or inclination to help us live in his image. It's false realism to think that we are hopelessly lost in a world in which Christian values cannot and should not be lived. We should never be afraid to cry out like the sinking Apostles: "Lord, save us, we perish" — no matter how sinful, no matter how neglectful our past life. And let us never forget that it was sinners that Christ came to save. "Though your sins be scarlet, they shall be made as white as snow."

We don't want to be Puritans or Jansenists; but we can't be sprites either, lurching ecstatically through life. Sometimes moral ineptitude may simply be inadvertence; but sometimes — if it damages other people's lives or our own — it can be actual sin.

The great sinner tends to be intense. The fury of Saul the Persecutor became the zeal of Paul the Apostle. The abandon of Magdalene the Sinner became the love of the Faithful Mary. They had intensity both as sinners and saints, and it's a question of determining what direction one goes. Our Lord, indeed, was critical of two classes of people: the lukewarm and the hypocrite. He called the Pharisees, as we remember, whited sepulchers who paraded virtue and practiced vice; and the lukewarm he labeled — in so many words — walking emetics.

But our Lord had no difficulty, it seems, in relating to sinners, and he considered forgiveness of sin a greater miracle than curing. Recall the incident in the New Testament when our Lord said, "Thy sins are forgiven thee." And of course people looked at him askance that a mere man would attempt to forgive sin. But in order that they would recognize that he had the power, our Lord cured the man's physical handicap. "Take up thy bed and walk" was, in a sense, a supplement to the forgiveness of sins.

Another thing to keep in mind is that our Blessed Lord did say to the woman taken in adultery: "Thy sins are forgiven thee." But he also said: "Sin no more." Our Lord forgave the impetuous Peter for his denial, and his forgiveness was there even for a despairing Judas, had it been sought. "Rend your hearts, not your garments," we read. Christ is the one who forgives and the one we should imitate, even when the act of forgiving and forgetting is not easy.

We can live by the Sermon on the Mount, or we can be selfish sinners. Still worse, we can be selfish sinners pretending to live by the Sermon on the Mount. But we can, despite the sinfulness of our past, ask to be made whole and strong and faithful in the Lord's service. So let us not passively accept the standards of the world from its foulmouthed movies, its crooked politics, its commercial deceits, or its dehumanizing values merely because they are so common. We are perhaps sinners, and we can be forgiven anything but the desire *not* to be forgiven.

We should recognize the potentiality that exists in ourselves to change what needs to be changed. We should try to do what we can do, when what we can do is what we should do. And if we make a mess of our lives — sometimes perhaps we will make a mess of it — let's ask a loving and forgiving Christ to illumine us, to help us, to strengthen us — not by pretending there is no such thing as sin, but by remembering that the saint is only the sinner who keeps on trying.

# Insensitivity

*S*EVERAL years ago, in its presentation of the mini-series *Roots*, the television industry gave us an interesting insight not only into slavery but also into the American character. The serialized version of Alex Haley's novel dealing with slavery and its accompanying brutalities reached over eighty million people and it was seen in nearly thirty-two million homes — which means that this program amassed one of the largest cumulative audiences for any single television program in history.

And of course its interest cut across racial lines and across age-groups. Black eighth graders of a local school were more horrified by the treachery of fellow blacks who betrayed their African brothers than by the more obvious brutalities perpetrated by whites. Older blacks tended to compare more soberly the disabilities of the five generations involved; but the entire country was fascinated by the episode in our nation's history when human beings were sold like cattle and worked like oxen. We wondered how a supposedly God-fearing, churchgoing people not only lived with such an inconsistency but also defended it militarily — and asked God's blessings on their arms as they did so!

Slavery was indeed the "peculiar" institution, as it was called. Of course our wonderment is always more profound when we're considering other people's faults. Of course we are right to lament the appalling institution of slavery; the insensitivity of a whole people brings home to us — removed as we are by more than a century — the truth that people can get used to injustices and systems that perpetuate them.

I'm not suggesting that you and I are responsible for what an Alabama plantation owner did over a century ago, merely because we have white skins; but it's just too easy to make the slave owner the only villain. We must not forget that the early query in Genesis — "Am I my brother's keeper?" — was not a rhetorical question.

Of course we're our brothers' keeper. There are two insensitivities, I think, to moral law and to daily practice. We are too often insensitive to the misery and destitution around us. We conveniently forget the spiritual and corporal works of mercy, not out of conscious malice, but because misery is something "out there" — and our immediate lives are not touched, our private worlds are not involved. And that is simply a kind of detachment that a Christian cannot legitimately practice.

Our Lord tells us that what we do to the least of our brethren we do to him, and this applies equally to acts of omission and commission in our own time. In human history there has been a curious ambivalence between faith and practice. I'm not speaking of faults committed out of weakness; what I'm speaking of is a curious piety that is meticulous in devotion but callous in practice.

Not too long ago a friend trying to get me by phone on a Saturday afternoon told of getting a wrong number, and a man snarled into the phone: "Don't bother me with your wrong numbers. I have to get to church." Kindness — elementary kindness — and going to church were somehow dissociated. Now, that kind of soulless fidelity is somewhat analogous to our games as children when we avoided walking on cracks in the sidewalk. Religion can become a ritualistic propriety rather than a *metanoia* (that is, a spiritual conversion) of mind and heart. We either live our Christianity or we don't, and if we are flanked by prejudice and hypocrisy we're simply too wide to get in that church door, and we might just as well stay home. But if we need God's help to make us see it, and if we need God's help to make us act as we know we should, let's ask humbly for God's help and be confident that he will give us that help.

If we watched, however, the concluding portion of *Roots* and said, "Thank God I'm not like the slave owner," it's like listening to the Gospel story of the publican and saying piously: "Thank God I'm like the publican."

113

Let's start our social and moral revolutions with ourselves. It's an enterprise that should keep us fairly busy. Then we can say, "Tsk, tsk, tsk" to those *bad* people out there.

# Distant Christians

*S*OME
time ago I was visiting on the West Coast a couple that I had married ten years earlier. They are attractive, successful; but — above all — they have acquired a great spiritual maturity, a fact that I commented upon.

The young wife phrased her answer well. "For most of my life," she said, "God was 'out there.' I was here, and though I went to church regularly and avoided sin, God was not really a presence in my life except for an occasional panic call."*

I think that describes many of us. God is too often the great "out there" — not our loving Father, not the joyous presence of inspiration, patience, and caring. We have made God the great bookkeeper in the sky, from whom we keep a comfortably respectful distance. And we do this with reasonable success, keeping his commandments but quite unable to relate to those saints of

---

*That young woman has since died, but she exhibited in her last illness an inspiring serenity of spirit, and a sense of "going home."

the infant Church who were transfixed and transformed by the Holy Spirit, consumed with the love of Christ, aware of God's continued presence and supportive love, possessed by the realization that charity for one's fellow-man meant translation of theory into practice.

My young friend went on to describe how her own discovery of a prayer life changed her life, as if she really were seeing Christ for the first time. She took that extra step to study and reflect on the Word of God, to ask God for the great gift of understanding, and to seek through the Eucharist an intimacy far removed from the minimal function of Christianity. She realized that we need the integration of supposedly removed prayer life really to become Christians and cope with life and its problems.

But what is "reality"? We are often shattered like the worldlings without faith, whose fragmented value system lacks wholeness and integration. I think that the reason our faith fails to give us that integrating vision is that we are almost afraid to become thoroughly convinced Christians for fear of the cost we might have to pay.

Like a fearful swimmer at the seashore, we hate to take the plunge into the chilly water, although we enjoy ourselves once we have taken the plunge. Some of us hover around a genuine faith most of our lives, instead of opening ourselves to the transforming fires of the Holy Spirit. So our faith does not really serve us very well. We are really secularists with a few Christian patches stuck on — and if we would change all that, we must be willing to let God operate in our lives.

We must build a daily prayer life around the great

centers of faith, hope, and charity. It is amazing how many of our problems do revolve around an absence of one or more of these great theological virtues. We must rediscover Sacred Scripture and read it before turning out that light each night. We must detach ourselves from an obsession with a society that is too acquisitive, too competitive, too materialistic, too selfish, and too uncaring. We must — most of all through the Eucharist — become more faithful models of the Christ we profess to love and serve.

The distant Christian finds it advantageous to remain at a distance. One of the most melancholy and poignant observations of the New Testament occurs after the seizure of Jesus in the garden of Gethsemane; we read that Saint Peter followed afar off. How often that is the story of our own lives. We follow — but afar off. We find it advantageous sometimes to remain at a distance, because we can maintain a proper public posture without looking too closely into our own lives.

The involved Christian opens up to God's grace, to the needs of his soul in his world — and, most of all, he realizes that he cannot kid himself into thinking that he is something that he isn't.

He doesn't use human frailty as an excuse for doing nothing to become more Christ-like. It's so comforting to be thought modest when all we are is lazy. God sees us as we are, and we should see ourselves as we are; and if we don't like what we see, we can try to become better. It's that simple — and that difficult.

116

# Sickness

*T*HE healing narratives of the liturgy are quite obviously not meant to be medical records but God's loving presence to a hurting people in a prescientific age. Christ's healing power was not limited to the ills of the body (as we learn from the narrative in which the paralytic is healed in both body and spirit, and his sins forgiven). Illness is something to which we can all relate, whether it comes in the form of acute distress, or in the form of inexplicable fatigue during that third set of tennis which in earlier years used to be so effortless.

By illness we are reminded of our frailty and mortality, and we know that for us — as for every man and woman — a final summons will come. Our Lord tells us that as his followers we are to pick up our crosses daily and follow him. But this need not mean that we can do nothing, if, in God's providence, we are ill. Winston Churchill once said that most of the serious work of the world is done by people who don't really feel very well.

Our Lord does have mercy on the multitudes, and on individuals when they find the way too steep or the road too rocky. God's loving presence, his healing presence, is still with his people. "Come to me all you who labor and are burdened and I shall refresh you."

From the most famous to the most insignificant, illness of body and spirit comes. And we all need the strength of spirit to see the infirmities of life in a proper context. Christ tells us, not that we shall be relieved of life's crosses, but that faith will give us strength and courage to bear them. I watch our blind students at the university, and I marvel, not only at their ability to move swiftly and confidently, but at their almost unfailing good humor. I marvel at a Helen Keller, an imprisoned intelligence that fought its way out of a sightless and soundless world. She was an incomparable witness to the courage and perseverance of the human spirit.

Most of us would be overwhelmed, at first, to be told that we no longer could look upon a sunset, a blue sky, a beautiful face, or see our loved ones grow; but illness like that is not something that happens to someone else. If our powers are diminished or our years shortened, we can survive. And as men and women of faith — who know that death is not the end — we can live our life with courage and grace and reasonable serenity, giving the days we have the qualities of love and considerateness that make for a good life. If we are bruised by sin, the healing power of a loving Lord can also be felt.

Interestingly enough, our Lord indicates in the New Testament that the forgiving of sin is a greater gift than the healing of bodies. And it was in order to convince the incredulous that he had the power to forgive sin, that he performed the most convincing and dramatic acts of healing — not only in the cases of Lazarus, the daughter of Jairus, and the centurion's servant but also in numerous instances involving blindness, deafness, leprosy, and epilepsy.

I remember visiting Lourdes some years ago and reading this sign: "The greatest miracle here is the prayerful acceptance in the hearts of those who are not cured." If our hearts are troubled, no matter how healthy we are, we are unhappy; and if we are inwardly at peace, then infirmity of the body can be tolerated without undue disturbance.

As we grow older, we recognize the inevitability of declining health and declining years; but as Saint Paul reminds us, we should not be depressed like the pagan who has no hope — and no faith. We should look with serenity at the passing stages of life, even if some of those stages are painful, for it is only to the faithless that death is oblivion and dissolution. Death for us is the portal to eternity. A loving God will indeed wipe all tears from our eyes and we shall be at peace. Our Lord was once asked by those very practical Apostles as to their reward and he told them very simply, "I will reward you a hundredfold and give you eternal life." Our Christ is not only the healing Christ, he awaits us at the end of the journey. He is our beginning and our end — and our hearts, however bruised by life, will be at peace.

We were recently given, in the last message of Terence Cardinal Cooke of New York, a wonderful example of what a Christian's attitude toward illness (among other things) should be: "The gift of life, God's special gift, is no less beautiful when it is accompanied by illness or weakness, hunger or poverty, mental or physical handicaps, loneliness or old age. Indeed, at these times, human life gains extra splendor, as it requires our special care, concern and reverence. It is in and through the weakest of human vessels that the Lord continues to reveal the power of his love."

# Generosity

$O_{UR}$ Blessed Lord was teaching one day in the temple, and he asked: "A man had two sons. He went to the first and said: 'My boy, go and work today in the vineyard.' 'I will, sir,' the boy replied, but he never went. The father came to the second and said the same. The second said, 'I will not.' But later, he changed his mind and went. Which of the two did his father's will?"

Though his hearers could sometimes be singularly obtuse, they caught the message. Forget the talk. Forget the promises. Forget the protestations, even denials. What you are actually doing is what is important. How are you performing? How does what you say relate to what you actually do? Now the second son was hardly perfect, but then nobody's son is. He grumbled, but he did his father's will — not graciously, but he did it. Ah, but the first son. The big talker. The promiser. Of course I'll go out there and work for dear old Dad. But he didn't. His words were so much more pleasant than his grumbling brother's; but he didn't perform.

The Christian life is not an oratorical contest. Even the bluff and hardy Peter talked a big game in saying he would never deny Christ. But he *did* deny Christ. The Christian life consists of trying to do Christ's will, not formulating words as to how we would like to do it, but doing it as best we can. And sometimes we're going to make a mess of it. So what does Christ tell us is the fundamental requirement of his way of life? How does he reduce it to its essentials?

He told us simply to love God and to do his will and to love our neighbor. He doesn't tell us to love mankind or humanity — and we have reformers today who love humanity but hate people. Many of the great talkers love humanity, but they're not so fond of rubbing elbows with individuals. And you know our Blessed Lord was rather literal when he spoke to the Apostles. I can remember once hearing a little girl, preparing for her first communion, describing the Twelve Apostles as the "Twelve Impossibles." In many ways they were simply that. They were impossible. They were sometimes rude. They were sometimes ambitious. They even had mothers who looked for preferential places for them in the kingdom of God. But they were still the vehicles by which Christ chose to make known his way to the world.

And who is my neighbor? It's not only that fellow next door who forgets to return my garden hose, and lets his dog roam on my front lawn. It's also — as Christ defines "neighbor" — the one who needs my love, the one who needs my help, the one who may be hurting, the one with whom I should share joy and sorrow. My neighbor is not only a son or a daughter or a loved one. He is the man who fell among thieves, the hurt, the sick, the starving, the lonely, the persecuted, the ignorant, the innocent. And he's not always the most gracious, or the most appreciative, or the most thoughtful. Sometimes those who are bruised by life — who spend their time trying to survive — never acquire the social graces that are the accouterments of a more affluent society.

There is a wonderful scene in the French film *Mon-*

121

*sieur Vincent*, in which Vincent de Paul tells the queen that those who are helped are not always appreciative. They are rarely gracious — because they are life's bruised ones. But that is no reason for not extending help, merely because the recipient is not sufficiently or appropriately appreciative. Some of us, I suppose, would wash the feet of our neighbor, only if we were sure that those feet were clean already. Christ doesn't tell us to help out the nice people. Gratitude has nothing to do with our Christian concern. It only makes us feel better, and that is not what it's all about.

This to me is the only setting that makes sense in discussing something like the appeals to charity that we get habitually. There is a need and we can help fill it. Such things as the Mental Health Association, the Apostolate to the Deaf, the Spanish Center, Foreign Missions — these are needs, to cite but a few. Should we simply write off the deaf, and tell them to go and read a book? Or should we try in a living liturgy to effect a detour around their infirmity, to prevent their drifting away? Hispanic Catholics in our midst have to be reached more effectively. Remember how the Irish immigrants in the nineteenth-century South drifted away? We must increase our Spanish-speaking apostolate to compete with the voices of the world, and the competing philosophies of secularism, or cultism, or simple infidelity.

As long as our brothers and our sisters out there need help of any kind, we react as Christians and do what we can, however we can, when we can, and as often as we can. And we will be asked frequently because the need continues to exist. Too often, appeals for help sound like someone is trying to sell a used car, or propose a green garden paradise in the Mojave Desert. An appeal for help, however, is not a hard sell or a soft sell or a sell at all; it's a call. Somebody out there needs us. And we are Christians. And so we help — even if our lesser selves identify these constant importunities as nuisances, which they are.

# Authenticity

*O*UR
Blessed Lord spent much of his time repudiating the empty formalism and legalism of the hypocrites of his day. He was often criticized by the self-righteous because he associated with tax collectors and prostitutes and other sinners. But he taught that empty formalism and attention to externals is simply not enough. He wanted his disciples then — and his disciples now — to be real and authentic religious personalities. Life, he seemed to think, is really too short to be anything else.

There is an old saying: "What you are speaks with such volume that I can't hear what you say." Today we hear the word "authenticity" quite often. So many of us pretend — that is, we play roles dictated by our culture.

By authentic I don't mean uninhibited in the sense of Rousseau's noble savage. To be natural is not to be rude and undisciplined. G.K. Chesterton used to say:

"Nature is not our mother but our sister." Nature is the handiwork of God's creative intelligence.

When I learned to fly, I was particularly struck by seeing the earth come to life in the springtime, or to see while traveling in Europe the majestic Alps as dawn broke on a Rome-bound plane. Or again, to see the ocean from a ship in early morning. There is a sense in which the self sometimes becomes aware of reality at its most basic.

What is this authenticity when we apply it to ourselves? I think, first of all, to be authentically human is to see and love God's children and God's world; to see the world's joy as well as its pain; to be a part of life rather than an aloof spectator; to be mature in the acceptance of our responsibilities, whether those responsibilities be official, familial, social, or personal. I think that sense of responsibility is closely linked to authenticity because we are so prone to evade responsibility by playing the role of some kind of Franz Kafka victim image.

The authentic person is not a whiner. He plans his life with reason, pursues his plans with perseverance, accepts defeat with grace, and enjoys victory with magnanimity. He sees life's pain as a part of the price of living, but his human solicitude and compassion try to minimize its ravages among the human family.

To be authentic is to recognize the limitations of self and others, and not to be overwhelmed by that knowledge. It is to try for perfection but at the same time to realize perfection's unattainability in this life. It is to avoid the paralysis of cynicism, even in the most difficult of times. It is to see the value of love and generosity in the human experience, to balance innovation and tradition. It is to cultivate the mind to the richness of truth and goodness and beauty.

To be authentic is to realize the relative shortness of our years and the need to fill those years with the best that is in us. It is to be possessed of the gentle humor that gives us the capacity to cushion much of the harshness of life by learning to laugh at ourselves when we get too pompous or solemn. It is to work conscientiously, to relax enough to enable us to function with efficiency and grace. It is to render to God the worship that is his by right, to realize that his Word must be translated conscientiously into our world so that home, marketplace, and nation may profit by our devotion. This world will be better or worse for our having been in it, and we also can determine what the verdict will be.

# Faith

*L*ORD, save us! We perish!" the impetuous Peter cries out in the Gospel. It is not only the cry of an apostle of faltering faith. In a sense, it is the cry of the human condition, and perhaps there comes a time in all but the most placid and unruffled of lives when we must and really should call out to the Lord to save us, to help us, to illumine us, to fortify us.

We live in an age of great cultural change, and the faith which is also a part of that changing culture does not always seem to be able to bring the stability and the confidence that it once did. It doesn't, because unbelief and a faltering faith make up such a big part of our contemporary world's cultural climate.

But in faith too we must not be unduly preoccupied with the miraculous, such as walking on water. We must distinguish what is changing and temporal in the faith — the cultural condition as it were — from what is permanent and essential, and we must make that permanent faith in the divine person of Jesus Christ both the religious and psychological center of our lives.

Christ reproved Peter as if to say, "Of course I will take care of you, no matter what. You know I won't let you sink. You know I promised you I would be there. You know that I have reminded you that the very hairs of your head are numbered."

Now, our Blessed Lord wasn't just making a promise to Peter. He was making a promise to us, to whom Peter was to preach, instruct, administer. That is the secret of the Gospels. We are meant to be participants, not mere spectators. The Gospels expect a resonance in our lives. We must not succumb to the fallacy of remoteness, which is to think Christ's love and help and Christ's values are too removed in time and space to be of any help to us in what we call the real world. To have faith is, in a sense, to despoil ourselves, to be poor and open to God's call.

Faith is not always security, but a risk. It is not always consolation, but a challenge. Faith is not resting, but being animated by perhaps a restlessness to see that

God's love and God's justice triumph in our world. Faith is an effort of the soul, and — in a sense — the soul never stops struggling against it. To have faith is to trust, to place oneself in the hands of someone else. Beyond our desire for freedom is the desire to love and to trust as sons to a father. We trust Christ and the instrumentality of the Church, not because we are perfect but because Christ is.

And sometimes — in a life which emphasizes worldly, acquisitive values — the life of faith may be momentarily dimmed, and we are fearful! But difficulty can coexist with faith. We are told that we see now darkly, but that eventually we will see in all true brilliance the light of truth. It is not scandalous to question. To ask a sincere question is itself an act of faith because it means believing that there is an answer that our Lord can give.

It has been said that every laboratory is a place of faith. Of course faith in its natural dimension is quite compatible with our human nature. However, when we're talking of it in a theological sense, faith is the first of the great three theological virtues of faith, hope, and charity; it is the human response to divine truth that is inculcated by the Gospels.

Now, why do we intensify our meaningful quest for truth in the world, and often abandon it in the quest of our life and happiness? We have our enchanted moments; but often we are overwhelmed by evil and sickness and mystery in the world, and our faith seems to weaken.

We must continue to love and to bleed and to hope, despite our infidelities and the instability of our very human hearts. We must continue to hope. We are children of our time, and we don't have much cultural help in an age in which faith is not strong.

The rock, of course, for us is a divine Christ. And the Church which he established is not just an organization but the human extension of a divine purpose in time. It will be run *by* men, not angels, *for* men, not angels.

And it will try to articulate God's will in the many contingencies of life, as well as to preserve the great inheritance that we call the Creed. And the articulation of that truth is sometimes a harder job than its preservation, but the Church will continue trying. The Church will love and suffer and try, and it will largely succeed, and it will bring its children home to him who alone is perfection, fulfillment, complete truth, and perfect love.

The Church's ministers will never, of course, be perfect; the people to whom it administers will never be perfect. But we must have patience with ourselves as well as with others in the living of the life of faith. We must have faith in commitment, though many commitments are flawed.

We must be men and women of integrity when a lack of integrity is both frequent and publicized and even advocated. We must be apostles of charity in an age that ridicules its impracticality. We must live this great paradox that is our faith. It will bring us home, and when we are there, faith will be no more, for we shall then possess and be possessed by faith's object.

# Toleration

*O*<small>NE</small>

of the most dubious compliments one can receive is to be told by a patronizing foreign acquaintance who thinks he is giving you the ultimate compliment: "You're not at all like an American." This suggests the intriguing question of what an American is really supposed to be like, if rudimentary civility and marginal literacy evoke such praise. It seems to be really a kind of relief on the part of the one giving the compliment that the American did not behave like a savage.

On the occasion when this happened to me, I gathered that an American was thought to be either a cowboy or an Indian, or a gum-chewing dead-end kid, who speaks in crisp, unintelligible prose, and has the traditional three-word vocabulary of the street. Perhaps as a people we have got over the passion we used to have to be liked all over the world. But I think that as a people we too have to learn tolerance, and perhaps we have to learn intolerance as well.

When I say intolerance, I mean intolerance of the "anything goes" philosophy so many of us who profess to be Christ's followers seem to have accepted. We should be intolerant of the viciousness which masquerades again as a legitimate option in today's society. Maybe intolerance which is the theme of the liturgy sometimes is neither as asinine or as obvious, but every society seems to have a convenient object of derision. We resent being patronized, but we often regard the foreigner and the stranger not as different but as inferior.

I would like to reiterate a story about taking a classmate with me to a lecture at the Sorbonne. He had a happily simple belief that if he repeated himself loudly enough in English, anyone in the world not a congenital idiot should be able to understand him. I remember how shocked he was that the lecture was in French, which I timidly suggested was not too unusual, since we were in Paris. The world is not really built around us, so we should be reasonably tolerant of diversity. But, as I say, we do not have to be tolerant of sin.

I think our Lord is teaching us tolerance in the obvious manifestation of charity, that we should avoid critical, facile generalizations about other races, other nations, other peoples, other cultures, other faiths. Toleration may not be Christian charity, but it's certainly a good start toward its acquisition. It is neither a permanent suspension of judgment nor the brutal suppression of one's critical faculties. But intolerance, I think, tends to be premature and unfair from a judgmental point of view. It's based on faulty sampling. Remember the shock of the Apostles when they saw our Lord talking to a Samaritan woman? They were not shocked because they knew of her many marriages; they were shocked because she was a Samaritan, and Jews did not speak to Samaritans — the latter having become a separate tribe and sect by the fourth century B.C.

But our Lord — in the parables of the Good Samaritan and the cured lepers — fought this trend. The disciples, quite simply, were to love their traditional enemy. Oddly enough, these enmities endure long after people have forgotten the reason for the estrangement. Whether it be a family feud, national, ethnic, or linguistic loyalty, that which divides peoples is condemned by our Lord. And essentially beyond the mindlessness of perpetuated animosity is the fact that we are all children of God. We are all made in the image and likeness of God with sovereign power to know and love and to decide. Our bodies — no matter what our condition culturally, ethnically, or financially — are temples of the Holy Spirit. We should have reverence for the godliness in self and in our neighbor — and that reverence should be spelled out behaviorally in a sense of self-respect that sees immediately the incongruity of certain forms of behavior with the Christianity that we possess. We should also see the incongruity of treating a fellow human being as a non-person, or as an inferior member of the species.

Christ tells us that we are to see him in our neighbor, and — as obvious as it is — it is something we practice so badly. In toleration we simply enlarge our vision. We see our brother and sister in everyone who exists, and we try as effectively as we possibly can to make that vision of Christ a reality.

So let us fret not if we are mistaken for ugly Americans. Sometimes — even frequently — we are. But we can try better not to be.